More Praise for Phil Bolsta's *Sixty Seconds*

"Life is made up of a series of moments, moments that often fly by without notice, vaporizing into the past. And yet, every once in a while, an experience seems to make time stand still. A mere moment has such a profound effect upon our lives that we are changed forever. Those moments are the ones we remember, reflect on, and carry with us. Phil Bolsta has put together a beautiful collection of just such moments, shared by some of the most accomplished and respected teachers of our time. This book, and the moving stories contained in its pages, is absolutely awesome. I love it!"

—**Lisa Marie Coffey**, author of *What's Your Dosha, Baby?*

"Wow! and double wow!! is what this remarkable book is! If you want to have an exclamation mark in your understanding of our world by some of the best living thinkers, teachers, speakers, leaders, and contributors to it . . . read this book now. You will thank me in your prayers for recommending it."

—**Mark Victor Hansen**, cocreator of *New York Times* bestselling series *Chicken Soup for the Soul*®, coauthor of *Cracking the Millionaire Code* and *The One Minute Millionaire*

"Phil Bolsta has captured the essence of life-changing and transformative moments from our culture's vision holders. This is a must-read for everyone who knows that life is a series of life-changing moments called the present."

—**Craig Neal**, cofounder of Heartland Inc., former publisher of *Utne Reader*

Sixty
Seconds

Sixty
Seconds

*One moment
changes everything*

collected by **Phil Bolsta**

foreword by **Caroline Myss**

ATRIA BOOKS
New York London Toronto Sydney

BEYOND WORDS
PUBLISHING

ATRIA BOOKS

A Division of Simon & Schuster, Inc.
1230 Avenue of the Americas
New York, NY 10020

PUBLISHING

20827 N.W. Cornell Road, Suite 500
Hillsboro, Oregon 97124-9808

Copyright © 2008 by Phil Bolsta

Managing editor: Lindsay S. Brown
Copyeditor: Henry Covey
Proofreader: Marvin Moore
Cover/interior design: Sara E. Blum
Composition: William H. Brunson Typography Services

First Atria Books/Beyond Words hardcover edition April 2008

ATRIA BOOKS and colophon are trademarks of Simon & Schuster, Inc.
Beyond Words Publishing is a division of Simon & Schuster, Inc.

Manufactured in the United States of America
ISBN-13: 978-1-58270-193-6

The corporate mission of Beyond Words Publishing, Inc.: *Inspire to Integrity*

To Erin
*For blessing me with a life filled
with sacred moments*

To Kate
*For your unwavering love and
support for this project*

To Mom
*For showing me how to love,
fully and unconditionally*

Contents

Part I: Glimpses into the Unknown   1

Life-and-Death Moments

Sacred Moments

Part III: Insightful Incidents 135

Life-Altering Moments

Moments of Enlightenment

Foreword

One of the great ironies in life is that as much as we might fear change, we constantly pray for our lives to change in some way. We recognize that change is constant—that nothing remains the same forever—yet we hold tight to the idea that change must be easily recognized and, above all, initiate minimal trauma. Another irony is that, even with all our fear of change, we believe that for something to make a lasting difference in our lives, it has to be grand, obvious, big, loud, and have a guaranteed outcome. We have an inherent mistrust of the subtle, much less anything that takes a while to come to fruition.

Yet, the truth is that the most meaningful events that have shaped our lives have, by far, been the smallest and the subtlest. Even within the greatest traumas of life, such as the loss of a loved one, a major accident, the sudden loss of a job, a divorce, or any of the other great sufferings of life, what is most remembered after the months pass and the individual begins speaking about the sorrowful event are the particularly healing or grace-filled inter-actions that occurred during the darkest of times.

A conversation with the right person at the right time has the power to reshape the whole of our life, and in fact, the whole of your life has been shaped in precisely this manner through events and encounters with significant individuals, the highlights of which lasted no more than sixty seconds. As a result of those sixty seconds, however, your life's path was profoundly redirected. Perhaps your encounter led to a spiritual awakening, or maybe it opened the passageway into the cosmic domain, which ultimately compelled you to examine the meaning and purpose of your own life. For some, their sixty-second moment broke through the barriers of heartaches and emotional wounds that prevented healings and the building of healthy adult relationships.

For the past few years, I have been deeply influenced by the work of Saint Teresa of Avila, who continually encouraged her nuns to "look for God in the details of your life." What, then, would God look like? God would manifest as these sixty-second encounters that hold such profound power that it can only be said that we emerge from them a different person. Ordinary moments in life—and there are far more of those—do not contain the grace that characterizes these sixty-second transformational moments. And this is the reason these stories deserve to be gathered together in this book.

One of my own stories is included in this wonderful book, my encounters with the holy avatar Sai Baba. While I had more than one sixty-second encounter with him, none were longer than a minute, and each one profoundly impacted my life. Indeed, I would have to say that I clung to the power of my encounters with Sai Baba as a lifeline, so extraordinary were those rare moments when they occurred.

I have always had the faith that our lives are not random events, that we matter to a Divine Being, but no matter how much faith we think we have, we are still filled with awe and wonder when a moment unfolds in our lives in which we awaken from within just long enough to recognize the presence of God in every detail of our life. One of those moments, as the many authors of these stories share, is enough to inspire a different life direction or dissolve any fears about living and dying.

The categories of stories in this book cover the best topics I can imagine in terms of the sixty-second transformation: life and death, the mysterious, heartbreak, the sacred, and enlightenment. Author and dear friend Phil Bolsta not only selected themes that are ideally suited to the power of grace, guidance, and sixty-second transformations, but he also selected extraordinary individuals to share their personal stories, all of which are heartwarming and inspiring.

But of all the benefits that you the reader will gain from this book—and there are many—I think the greatest is the message of how quickly your life can change and how little it takes for heaven to initiate that change. Most often, you are looking in the wrong direction for your life to change, fearing dragons and sea monsters that are never going to show up on your doorstep. Rather, the Divine reveals itself to you in the subtle events, conversations, and experiences of your life—in potent sixty-second encounters that leave you breathless and filled with awe. That is the signature of God.

Ask anyone who has had a near-death experience that, according to the clock, was no longer than sixty seconds. That person returns to his body not only certain that death does not exist, but he also knows that he will be greeted by his loved ones and embraced by an intimate and loving Light that knows all the details of his life down to the first word he uttered as a child. This is not the result of a car accident or a man's imagination during surgery to repair his damaged body. This man encountered God during his near-death experience for less than sixty seconds, yet those sixty seconds were the most authentic of his earthly life.

I have no doubt that every reader will be blessed by the experience of reading *Sixty Seconds: One Moment Changes Everything*. And further, I would bet that after reading this wonderful book, no one will ever take one minute of life for granted again. You just never know what the next moment may bring.

Caroline Myss
author of *Entering the Castle* and *Anatomy of the Spirit*

Acknowledgments

I am indebted to the forty-five storytellers in this book and grateful for their generosity, kindness, and willingness to share their personal stories.

Special thanks to my homegrown editors. Kate Moore, the mother of my daughter, was my staunchest supporter and contributed many helpful suggestions. Erin Moore, the best daughter ever, spent many hours combing through the stories and offering insightful fixes. Friend Susan Foster, a true professional with superior editorial skills, was also a big, big help.

A special thank-you to my agent, Barbara Deal Neighbors. I wish everyone I worked with shared her caring nature and upbeat attitude.

I was blessed to work with a phenomenal publishing team. Cynthia Black, Richard Cohn, Lindsay Brown, Marie Hix, and Rachel Berry of Beyond Words took my work and elevated it to a higher level than I ever dreamed possible.

Introduction

I t was a beautiful March day. But when I picked up the phone I knew that somebody somewhere was dying. It was Ann Lutgen, an Allina Hospice coordinator. As a hospice volunteer and certified massage therapist, I get called when a terminally ill patient is in need of healing touch. "We have a fifty-eight-year-old man with lung cancer," Ann said. "He's having trouble breathing, which causes him to panic. His family thought massage might help."

"Sure, I can see him in the next few days," I told her. "What's his name?"

When Ann said, "Charles Potuznik," I froze. *Oh, my God*, I thought. *That has to be Chuck.*

Twenty-two years earlier, I had worked for a volatile entrepreneur who produced a monthly newsletter to tout the investment value of the rare coins he sold. We had retained Chuck Potuznik, a savvy attorney from a well-regarded law firm, to approve the text. At Chuck's urging, I looked into a newsletter story claiming that we had purchased a large cache of coins from the estate of a wealthy collector out West. I discovered that the story had been fabricated and told Chuck this on the phone. He was appalled. "If you're going to tell these Little Red Riding Hood stories," he said, "I can't be a party to it." He resigned on the spot. As soon as I found another job, I quit too.

I hadn't seen or spoken to Chuck since. But even before that final conversation, he had made an indelible impression on me. It's rare, but something just clicks into place when you meet certain people. They enter your orbit, and you enter theirs. I think I only met Chuck once and spoke to him a handful of times, but in the years that followed, his name would flash in neon letters in my mind whenever I'd see a "Best Lawyers in the Twin Cities" article or overhear a conversation about corporate attorneys.

The impact Chuck made on me never faded and, in fact, may have grown stronger as time passed. I didn't have a clue why, but I sensed that our paths would cross again. After Ann's phone call, everything tumbled into place, and peacefulness settled over me. It all made perfect sense. The time had come to complete the circle of energy that connected us.

A few days later, I arrived at Chuck's house and was ushered to his bedroom by a family friend. Chuck was lying in bed, weak but mentally sharp. He couldn't be moved, so the best I could do was reach behind him to massage his neck and shoulders. "That feels incredible," he murmured as I worked.

After a couple minutes, I said, "You know, Chuck, you and I go way back." He tilted his head toward me and managed a curious smile and a subtle nod of the head—an invitation to continue.

I told him we had worked together way back when and that he had resigned the account in a phone conversation with me. "Tell me that story," he whispered. I did, adding that I had always considered him a model of integrity. In fact, I told him, a number of years ago, I had made a commitment to live my life with complete integrity, no matter the cost. He smiled and nodded again. As I massaged his back and arms, we spoke of the importance of living with integrity and of treating each person we encountered with love and compassion. I gently massaged him for more than an hour. Everything about our time together that day felt right. I told him I'd be back soon.

Two days later, I visited Chuck again. The pain had worsened, so he was drugged and drifting in and out of consciousness. Still, he moaned in appreciation as I massaged his neck and back.

While I was rubbing him, I looked around the room. On the bedside table to my right was a photo of Chuck and his brothers, Wayne and Ken, on their last fishing trip together. Adorning the bureau and walls were photos of Chuck's wife, Mary, and their two adolescent daughters, whom he adored. Outside the window, the afternoon sun shone down on the placid waters of Lake Minnetonka. Chuck's world was filled with great love and beauty, yet his capacity to enjoy it was rapidly shrinking.

As I stood behind him, massaging his forehead, I whispered, "God bless you, my friend." I didn't think he'd heard it, but some part of him did.

From his stupor, he blurted out, "Wha?"

A little louder this time, I repeated, "God bless you, my friend." Eyes closed, he nodded his head and grunted in acknowledgment.

At one point, he haltingly lifted his hand and swiped at his nose with his little finger, then dropped his arm heavily back to his side. The area under his nose had been bloodied from oxygen tubes, so his finger was smeared with blood. I picked up his hand and, as I gently wiped his finger with a tissue, marveled at the twists and turns that life can take. Not that long ago, I had been a green twenty-five-year-old, respectfully deferring to a high-powered attorney eleven years my senior. Now here I was, comforting him and caring for him in his final hours. I felt honored to be at his side and thankful for the divine force that had brought us together one more time. Three days later, Chuck passed away.

I think of Chuck often. Simply by living his life, Chuck not only inspired me to be a better man, he deepened my faith and provided me with a profound glimpse into the mysteries of the universe. The moments I spent at his bedside were sacred, and I will cherish them always.

Odds are that you've experienced your own sacred moments. After all, more than half of adult Americans have experienced a spiritual transformation, according to the National Opinion Research Center (NORC) at the University of Chicago. Such transformations lead to dramatic changes in how people view themselves, the world, and the meaning and purpose of life.

These transformative experiences are available to us all. As the NORC study documents, these powerful, life-shifting events are typically triggered by either a personal crisis or a normal religious activity. Consequences typically include a strengthening of faith as well as positive, far-reaching changes in character, attitude, and behavior.

My own spiritual awakening was a gradual one. In my late twenties, I started thumbing through Shirley MacLaine's book *Out on a Limb*, and that was that. I was hooked. I wanted to experience those incredible epiphanies for myself. Most of all, I desperately wanted to achieve "enlightenment." Over the next few years, I devoured dozens of spiritually minded books, tapes, and seminars.

Then something thrilling happened. It was the Fourth of July. I was home alone. Work had prevented me from joining my wife, Kate, and daughter, Erin, on our traditional trip to northern Minnesota. We rarely missed a Fourth of July celebration in Kate's hometown.

Early that afternoon, I lay down on the bed to close my eyes and mentally sketch out the rest of my day. Two minutes later, I heard Kate's voice cheerfully calling out, "Hi, Phil!" Her greeting was loud and clear, as if she were standing right in front of me. The kicker was, I heard her voice inside my head.

I was stunned. I had always dismissed reports of "hearing voices" as a sign of mental illness. Yet there was no mistaking what had occurred. I had *heard* Kate's voice—not with my ears but with some unknown sense. I remember thinking, *So that's what that feels like. Cool!*

When Kate called the next day, I asked her what she had been doing at the time I'd heard her voice. She said, "Hmmm, oh, a bunch of us were sitting on the dock at Bev and Bill's cabin. Someone said, 'It's too bad Phil had to stay home,' and I said, 'Let's all say hi to him!' So we all shouted, 'Hi, Phil!' at the same time. Why? Did you hear us?" I shivered and told her that, yes, I had. "Oh, my God!" she said. "I can't believe it!" We were so excited, we had to go over the details again and again until we calmed down.

From that day on, my hunger for all things spiritual intensified. But the more I learned, the more I understood that spirituality isn't about cool parlor tricks. Ultimately, it's about how you choose to relate to the people and world around you. As my awareness grew, so did my capacity to recognize the sacredness in every moment. It eventually dawned on me that every day is a gift—and that what we do with it is our gift to ourselves, to others, and to the world.

When I felt I had grown enough to competently articulate these powerful truths to others, I set out to interview the authors and speakers whose work had resonated with me. I asked them to recall a profound moment in their lives when they felt deeply connected to spirit. I wrote up their stories for *Edge Life*, a Minneapolis-based magazine devoted to personal growth, integrative healing, and global transformation. Before I knew it, I had built up an impressive collection of wonderfully uplifting stories.

These intimate, life-altering stories of spiritual awakening and growth, rich with insight and meaning, remind us that everything we think, say, and do matters. Call it karma, or cause and effect, or what goes around comes around. Every action—from Stephen Simon approving a videotape delivery to Caroline Myss sending out a prayer to an Indian mystic to Christiane Northrup observing her first live birth—creates an unending sequence of ripples in the lake of our daily lives.

Not every story emerged from joyous occasions. Deepak Chopra, Joan Borysenko, and Dannion Brinkley were profoundly affected by the death of a parent. Echo Bodine made the heart-breaking decision to give up her only child for adoption. Frank Deford's daughter, Alex, was slowly, agonizingly consumed by cystic fibrosis. From them, we learn that, despite our hurt and our grief, every tragedy eventually reveals its own sacred purpose.

Even when these profound moments of spiritual clarity appear to affect nobody but ourselves—Dan Millman's spontaneous awakening while peeling a grapefruit, Tom Gegax's startling vision in a Greek hotel, Jean Houston's opening of a spiritual doorway—their consequences will echo through eternity. How? When people are changed by sacred experiences, the way they show up in the world changes too, which in turn subtly changes the people with whom they interact. Millions of us have already been jolted awake by one of these "life quakes." More minds and hearts are opening every day. Soon, we will reach critical mass, and our culture will be forever changed.

Is there a common thread among these stories? No, not really. Some are subtle and insightful while others are knock-your-socks-off amazing. I hope these stories will touch your heart as they have touched mine. Some of them may challenge you to rethink perceptions about the way the world works. Others may inspire you to make better life choices. Cumulatively, they may motivate you to live in a way that increases your awareness of the sacred moments that currently lie just beyond your vision.

Keep in mind that you don't have to wait for sacred moments to come to you. Create your own by listening to your heart. Years ago, when my daughter was young, I'd stand in the doorway to her bedroom and watch her sleep. I'd close my eyes and imagine she was eighteen, pulling out of the driveway, headed for college. As I watched her wave and drive off, I'd pray with all my heart that I could turn back time and spend just five more minutes with her when she was a wee sprout. Then I'd open my eyes and there she was, still my little girl, and we didn't have just five minutes, we had years! I practiced this "imagine the future" exercise well into her teenage years. Regularly reminding myself that her adulthood was fast approaching helped me cherish every minute we had together. Erin is now a lovely young woman, and those precious moments in her doorway will always stay with me.

Such sacred moments add depth and meaning to our lives. There is much you can do to prepare yourself for a transformational experience of your own. Get to know yourself better by reading self-help books. Keep a journal of your innermost thoughts. Meditate. Practice affirmations. Share your feelings openly and honestly with others. Most importantly, reflect each day on your opportunities for growth. And if all else fails, try standing in a doorway and counting your blessings.

Best of luck to you on your journey, my friend. May your life be long and prosperous, and may your days be filled with sacred moments.

Part I

GLIMPSES INTO THE UNKNOWN

> *It is one of the commonest of mistakes to consider
> that the limit of our power of perception is
> also the limit of all there is to perceive.*
> C.W. Leadbeater

B eyond the veil bordering the material world lie mysteries that our senses cannot grasp, that reason is unable to explain, that science cannot prove. And yet, startling evidence of paranormal phenomena showers down upon us unceasingly. All we need do is lower the umbrella of resistance and let the rains of enlightenment wash over us, cleansing our mind and awakening our soul.

These otherworldly experiences may be as subtle as the wind whispering in our ear or as spectacular as an out-of-body experience. As *The Course in Miracles* states, there is no order of difficulty in such events, which are often cloaked in the disguise of ordinary moments. This explains why *miracle* is a word used only by people who do not understand how the universe operates.

"Glimpses into the Unknown" is divided into two parts. "Life-and-Death Moments" includes unexplainable stories of lives saved or nearly lost and the secrets of life after death. Stories appearing in "Mysterious Moments," while just as inscrutable, deal with less urgent topics—visions, healings, and amazing happenings that defy the laws of physics.

1

JANIS AMATUZIO, M.D.

Known as the "compassionate coroner," Dr. Amatuzio writes and speaks about her personal experiences and insights regarding life after death and how to apply those lessons to live a richer, more rewarding life. The founder of Midwest Forensic Pathology, P.A., a company offering private autopsy services, she serves as coroner and provides forensic pathology services for several counties in Minnesota and Wisconsin. She has authored Forever Ours: Real Stories of Immortality and Living from a Forensic Pathologist *and* Beyond Knowing: Mysteries and Messages of Death and Life from a Forensic Pathologist. *For more information, visit www.foreverours.com.*

Back in 1978, I was in my last month of my internal medicine internship and doing a rotation at the University of Minnesota Hospital, working a grueling schedule of thirty-six hours on and twelve hours off. Thank God I was in my twenties, because I couldn't do that now! One night, I nodded off to sleep at 2 AM but it didn't last long. At 2:30, a nurse called and said, "Doctor, we need you to get up and start an IV for a man whose IV catheter dislodged. He needs a heparin infusion."

I considered myself a pretty seasoned intern by then, having spent eleven months at it. I said, "Tell you what, hot-pack it [to make the veins more pronounced] and call me in thirty minutes." I really, really wanted that extra thirty minutes of sleep.

The nurse knew I had a habit of sleeping through phone calls, so thirty minutes later she strode into the room, flipped on the light, stood at the foot of the bed, and said, "Get out of bed *now*, Dr. Amatuzio. This man's arm has been hot-packed for thirty minutes and he's waiting for you."

Exhausted and half-conscious, I dragged myself out of bed, grabbed a couple IV catheters and a tiny 25-gauge butterfly catheter, and trudged down the hall. I remember being envious because I could hear people snoring. There's a certain intimacy to 3 AM in a hospital ward. As you walk down the halls, it's quiet, dark, and the only sound you hear is rhythmic breathing. I could see in the distance that one of the rooms had a light on. I walked around the corner and into the room. The light coming from the ceiling made a cone over my patient, Mr. Stein, who was in the bed closest to the door.

When I looked at him, my heart sank. He was a very large man and was immensely swollen. The only thing that looked bright about him was his eyes. I thought, *How am I ever going to start an intravenous catheter quickly on this poor man?*

I sat down next to the bed and unpacked the moist hot packs from his arm. Since men don't have as much subcutaneous fat as women do, they usually have good veins that are close to the surface. But I couldn't see a vein anywhere on his arm, so I had to try to find one by palpation.

I introduced myself and told him I had to start a catheter. As I was feeling for a vein, this man looked at me and said, "You know, doc, I died once." My first thought was, *Whoa, he's off his rocker. He's sundowning.* He read my thoughts like he was reading a book and said, "You don't believe me," with such sadness that I was terribly embarrassed.

I said, "It's not that I don't believe you, but you know that's a pretty extraordinary thing you just said."

He said, "I know. But I did."

While I was feeling for a vein, I thought, *Well, I'm going to be here a long time; I might as well hear a good story*. So I asked him to tell me what had happened.

He said, "Well, you know I've got blood clots in my legs and they like to travel up to my lungs."

"I know," I said, "that's why it's so important to get this medication into your veins." He told me he had had a filtering screen put in his interior vena cava, the large vessel that brings the blood from the lower extremities up to the heart, to stop the clots from passing to his lungs.

"That was two years ago," he said. "And that's when I died."

I nodded. "Yeah, but you're here now."

"Yep, I came back to life." I felt a shiver go down my neck and remember thinking, *What is this?* But he looked so earnest. He told me that when the doctors had finished implanting the screen in his heart, which had taken five hours, he had been wheeled into the PAR (post-anesthesia recovery room). "I remember laying there, trying to come to consciousness," he said. "A nurse was squeezing my shoulder, trying to awaken me, but I just couldn't quite wake up."

By this time, I had palpated for a vein, found one, and was taping on the IV. "Then the strangest thing happened," he said. "All of a sudden, I left my body."

I looked at him and asked, "And *how* did you do that?"

He said, "Right through the top of my head."

"*Really?*" I said.

He said, "I remember looking down at my body from the ceiling. And I had such a sense of compassion for my body; I felt really sorry for it. All of a sudden, I noticed that the doctors and nurses were all rushing to my bedside. That puzzled me because I felt absolutely fine. But the most amazing thing was that I could hear all their thoughts. I could feel their concern; I could feel their love—except for one nurse, who was upset because she had a date after work and my cardiac arrest was delaying her. It was *amazing*. I went to the doctor's side and tapped him on the shoulder. He didn't feel me so I got right in front of him and tried to grab his arms. I said, 'Stop all of that, I'm fine.' But he didn't hear me."

"You could really hear every thought they had?" I asked incredulously.

"Yes," he said, "it was like reading their minds. And I watched them work furiously on my body. I watched them bring the paddles out and open up my gown to expose my chest. I saw my body jump every time they shocked me." I was already staring at him in disbelief, but he was just getting warmed up. "And then the most amazing thing happened," he said. "The man in the bed next to me, he had a cardiac arrest!"

"I suppose he left through the top of his head, too?" I asked.

"Yep," he said, "and was he ever surprised to see me!"

I laughed and asked what the two of them did next. He said, "Well, I communicated with him by just thinking and told him what had happened. When we realized we couldn't communicate with the doctors and nurses, we watched them work on our bodies for a while. There was only one crash cart and they had used most of the supplies on me. I watched the doctor shock me, turn around and shock him, turn back and shock me, then shock him again, and so forth. We saw them call for another crash cart. It was absolute havoc down there. Finally, we decided to leave. I know it sounds odd, but we really didn't feel attached to our bodies."

I had the IV in by now and had taped it down, but I was hooked on his story, even though it was now 3:30 in the morning. In my typical twenty-something fashion, I said, "And *how* did you do that?"

He said, "Doc, you're not going to believe this, but we just *thought* our way through the wall."

I said, "You *thought* your way through the wall?"

"Yep," he said, "we didn't go through a door or a window, we just thought ourselves through the walls and into the next room."

"Where did you end up?" I asked.

"In the waiting room. There were several people sitting there, and I could feel their concern for the well-being of their loved ones. But we couldn't communicate with them either, so we decided to leave the hospital."

"Did you use the elevator this time?" I asked.

He smiled. "No, we just thought our way through the hospital wall. I remember looking back and seeing the red brick and mortar."

"Well, what happened then?" I asked. "I mean, you're here now."

"Doc," he said, "when we got outside it was nice and warm and comfortable. And then ... I saw it." He paused for a moment to collect himself. With tears streaming down his cheeks, he said, "Off in the distance I saw—no, I felt—the most amazingly beautiful light. It was so bright, and it was made up of every color of the rainbow and more. I was instantly drawn to it and so was my companion. As we approached it, I felt the most incredible joy and awe and sense of grandeur I've ever experienced. Then, the light opened up into a tunnel. I felt a rush as I moved through it. It was like standing in an enormous wind," he said, pausing to gesture at my long hair, "only your hair wouldn't blow. When I got there, it burst open into a magnificent display of colors; colors I had never seen before even though they seemed so familiar.

"And then, I saw my mother and my father and my brother who had all died in an accident forty years ago. My dog was there too. I was overjoyed. It was a wonderful reunion. As I traveled upward toward the source of all this joy, I grew more aware. The brilliant dazzling colors shimmered, and I began to realize, well, *everything*. I can't explain it. I saw my life in its entirety, and I saw that everything that had happened to me had been perfect. Then suddenly, I knew with crystal clarity that I couldn't stay and why."

He paused again, so I asked, "Well, what happened then?"

He said, "You know that other guy?"

I said, "Yeah?" And he said with an absolutely distraught voice, "The other guy got to go on and I had to come back." And he just wept.

After a few moments, he was able to compose himself. He confided that he hadn't told that entire story to anyone before, that he had been afraid to talk about it. I squeezed his hand and thanked him for sharing his story. We sat there together in silence for a minute or two, sharing the intimacy of his story and of the early morning hours.

Finally, he spoke again. "When I got back, everything in my body hurt. My chest was burned from the paddles; my ribs were broken from the CPR; there were needle puncture marks everywhere on my body. But even though everything hurt, I was filled with an overwhelming sense of peace that I had never experienced before or since. When I was up there, with my family, I had been overwhelmed and stunned by the loving kindness that surrounded me.

"The next day, in the recovery room, my doctor told me what had happened—I had had a heart attack, and they had almost lost me. I didn't say anything, but a month later, I went to see him for a checkup and told him about my experience. I was still experiencing that sense of incredible peacefulness and purpose. I told him about leaving my body through my head, about floating up near the ceiling, about watching him try to resuscitate both me and the other guy, about that wonderful light.

"The doctor looked confused. All he could say was, 'You must have had a reaction to a medication.' I said, 'No, it wasn't a reaction, it was the most real thing that has ever happened to me.' And the doctor said, 'Listen, you don't know what you're saying. You were dead, dead and gone for fifteen minutes. Your heart wasn't pumping. Then, *bango*, your heart started again, and here you are.' I said, 'Doctor, I watched you during that resuscitation. I saw the man in the bed next to me die too. You only had one crash cart and not enough medications, and you were using the same set of paddles on both of us. And I felt how worried, frustrated, and concerned you and the staff were.'

"He shook his head and said, 'Absolutely impossible. You could not have known any of that. You were unconscious. The nurse must have told you.' He held up his hand and said, 'You know what, I don't know what you believe, I don't know what happened to you, but for all intents and purposes you were dead.' And I said, 'I know.'"

I looked at the clock. It was almost 4 AM. I sat there for a few minutes. And then I asked, "Did it change your life?"

"Oh, yes," he said, "in several ways. First of all, I don't fear death. I know we don't die. The experience that the doctor called dying was the most magnificent thing that's ever happened to me. Secondly, I know that love is all that counts. I still love my stuff, my things, but they don't matter to me the way they did before. It's who we're *being* that matters, not what we're *doing*. And lastly, I try to learn something each day, to gather knowledge, and then try to apply it to make this world, my world, a better place."

After that, he was very quiet. I remember how embarrassed I felt that I had doubted him. I told him that I believed him and the incredible journey he had taken. And I remember thinking, *I'm going to remember this wisdom*. And I have. It's made a difference in my life. It's helped me to remain sensitive to patients and their families. And when my loved ones die, it comforts me to know that it will not simply be the end, that we will all be together again someday.

2

JOAN BORYSENKO

Joan Borysenko has written thirteen books, including Minding the Body, Mending the Mind; Inner Peace for Busy People: 52 Simple Strategies for Transforming Your Life; *and* Your Soul's Compass: What is Spiritual Guidance?, *the latter coauthored by her husband, Gordon Dveirin. Borysenko was trained as both a medical scientist and a psychologist. Her vision is to bring science, medicine, psychology, and spirituality together in the service of healing. For more information, visit www.joanborysenko.com.*

My mother died when I was in my early forties. The day of her death, the family came together to keep a deathbed vigil. She was bleeding internally so they took her away for a test. The whole day passed, but she didn't return. I went to look for her and found that she had been lying on a gurney outside of the department of nuclear medicine all day. We had an exchange with a doctor there which turned out to be pretty funny. I said, "This won't do. She's dying. She needs the comfort of her family."

And the doctor said, "We need a diagnosis."

My mother, who was so weak, rallied herself, got up on her elbow, looked him in the eye and said, "You need a diagnosis? I'm dying; that's your diagnosis."

So I stole her. I started wheeling her away and said, "You're not having any tests. I'm taking you back to your room."

And he said, "Wait, the hospital rules state that an orderly has to take her."

I said, "Nobody's taking her, just me," and I wheeled her into the elevator to take her back to her room.

She looked at me and said, "We may not have much time left, and I want you to know one thing: I love you. I know that as a mother I've made a lot of mistakes, and I'd like to know that you can forgive me." In that moment, years of misunderstanding faded away, and there we were on the most profoundly sacred ground. It gave me a chance, not only to forgive her, but also to ask her forgiveness for being so filled with my own narcissism and judgments. It was the closest moment of our lives, that short ride in the elevator.

When we got back to her room, we were in a whole other landscape of being with one another, and I asked her something that I never would've asked under normal circumstances. I asked if she would exchange a soul quality with me. She was a very straightforward woman, but she got it right away. She looked at me and said, "I have always admired your compassion," which touched me deeply because I felt I had never really been compassionate with my own mother. I told her that what I admired most in her was her tremendous courage. This was a woman, like many of her generation, who had lived through very difficult times like the Great Depression and the death of many relatives in Auschwitz. But like many women in difficult circumstances throughout the world, she knew how to keep on going.

Not long after that, we started the countdown because she was getting weaker and weaker. In the middle of the night, my twenty-year-old son, Justin, and I were sitting by her bed meditating when I suddenly had a very profound, very realistic vision. I was a pregnant mother giving birth, but I was also the baby being born. Throughout the vision, I was perfectly lucid, and I was in my regular state of consciousness as well. I thought, *How remarkable. I'm in two bodies, and I'm conscious of being in both.*

And it occurred to me that that's what the consciousness of God is, and that it's present in every human being. Then, my consciousness switched totally into the baby being born, and I found myself coming down a long, dark tunnel and out into the light. Once I was in the light, I saw my entire relationship with my mother unveiled in an infinite number of layers. I saw that it had been absolutely perfect and that we had learned lessons from one another that had made us both more courageous and compassionate. I felt an overwhelming sense of gratitude for this woman. I also felt the circularity of things, that she had given me physical birth and, in this moment, I was giving birth to her soul as it was leaving.

When the vision was over and I returned to the room, my sight had changed. Instead of seeing things as solid objects, I saw everything as energy—it looked like everything was made of light and interconnected. And I saw that the energy of her now lifeless body was the same as the energy of the bed, the ceiling, the floor. I looked over at my son, who was sitting on the opposite side of the bed. It looked like he had a halo. He was crying. He looked at me with such a soft look in his eyes and said, "Mom, the whole room is filled with light. Can you see it?" I told him I could, and I moved around the bed and sat next to him.

He said, "I just had a vision. You must be extraordinarily grateful to Grandma Lily."

I said, "Yes, I am. For the first time in my life, I really know what gratitude is."

He said, "What I understood in my vision is that she was a very great soul, and she came to earth not for her own purposes but as a gift to you—so that in resisting her, you could become who you truly are, and you could develop the gift that you have to give to other people." At that point, Justin and I fell into one another's arms and began weeping.

I said to him, "I've made a lot of mistakes as a mother. Will you forgive me?"

"Of course," he said. And then, almost jokingly, he added, "You know, what I saw in my vision is that you must have wounded me in just the right way so that I could develop my own strengths."

I had dreams about my mother every night after she died for about a month. A couple weeks after her death, I had an extraordinarily lucid dream about courage. I found myself high up in the mountains in the company of a group of older women. They said they were in a school for spying, with the word *spy* meaning "to see clearly." I saw the strength and the courage of these women, and I wanted to have it too. I told them I wanted to join them, and they accepted me into their school. The day of the final exam, I lost track of my class and went wandering outside where I found a huge tree that was hollow in the bottom—I knew somehow that this was my final exam. With complete courage, I jumped into the hole. As I did so, a yellow inflatable raft materialized under me, and I went speeding through other planes of consciousness. I came out into the divine light and again had a clear sense of the safety, the meaning, and the interconnectedness of everything.

When I woke up that morning, I went to make coffee. There by the coffeemaker was a little red sticker about three inches across with swirly white letters. At first glance I thought it said *Coca-Cola*, but when I picked it up and looked closer I saw that it said *Courage*. And I thought, *My God, it's the Red Badge of Courage!* When my husband and son woke up later, neither of them said they had ever seen it before. I was reminded of people who talk about *apport* from the spirit world, where things from that world manifest directly into this one. And I thought, *That was my mother's soul promise to me, that she would give me courage.* In those times when my courage flags, I think of that experience and of my mother's gift to me.

3

JOSEPH COSTA, Ph.D.

Costa is founder of the World Healer Institute and the Institute of Thought in San Diego, California. A doctor of philosophy in psychology, he is the discoverer of the "human body brain" and is an authority on psychic phenomena, altered states, and mysticism. A member of the International Association for Regression Research and Therapies, Costa conducts seminars all over the world to teach the 15th Step process, a method that people can use to access the inner world, talk intimately with ascended masters, and receive divine answers and healing. Costa's books include Bringing the Eagles of Consciousness to the World; Primal Legacy: Thinking for the 21st Century; *and* The Second Coming of Yeshu. *For more information, visit www.15thstep.com.*

My guides first appeared when I was four years old. All of a sudden, these four old guys were in my bedroom. At first, I figured they were my uncles because I had a big family. It was the 1920s. We didn't have electricity, so they would light up the room and play games with me. They showed up almost every night after everyone had gone to sleep. I could hardly wait until everybody quieted down because I knew they were coming.

After a year or so, they started showing me how to consciously move energy along created "wires." If I concentrated really hard, I could move the energy from a created "power source" up to what I'd describe now as a giant TV screen in the middle of my ceiling. I could watch anything I wanted on it, from Tarzan movies to real-time viewing of my relatives who lived nearby.

When I was around six, I got my first clue that these beings weren't "real" people. I was working on bringing some energy along the lines because they always made me work to get the screen on. I was almost to the screen when a guide with red hair and a red beard standing by the end of my bed said, "Joseph can't do that." That was the first time one of them said I couldn't do something. It startled me and I lost control of the energy. I looked at him and said, "Yes, I can do that."

I focused back to the corner where the power source was, brought the energy along the circuitry, and got it right up to the screen. Again, he said, "Joseph can't do that," and boom, I lost it again. I got mad and said angrily that I could do it. I tried once more and the same thing happened. When he said, "Joseph can't do that," I jumped out of bed, ran at him, and punched him in the stomach. But my fist went right through him and hit my dresser. It scared the beejesus out of me. My hair stood on end and I ran back into bed and whimpered.

When I looked up, they were gone. I wasn't too sure I wanted them to come back, but of course I really did. From then on, I often was tempted to reach out and touch the ones who were closest to me. Then one night, one of them sat down at the foot of my bed and sank down. I could feel him against my feet, and I thought, *Oh, this one's real.*

My guides visited me regularly until I grew up and went into the Army. But even then, I always knew that they were there. I would often hear them, which was reassuring, and I didn't worry about my safety. I didn't actually see them again until I was in action and got into trouble.

Our combat outfit was armored with machine guns and cannons. We would shell the line heavily, the Germans would be shook up, and then we'd run through the line with two tanks, two half-tracks (semi-tanks that were half truck and half tank), and all the infantry. We'd get behind the German lines, take a strategic position, and hold it.

One night, when it was raining and pitch-black, our tank threw a track and we were stranded and exposed in a big rutabaga field. A German gun was shooting shells that were landing all around us. It was just a matter of time before they got us. I got mad and told the guys I was going out to get that SOB. I took a Thompson (machine gun), jumped out, and slammed the door shut. As I turned around, the world exploded. Next thing I knew, I was in a ditch 150 feet away. Shells were coming in and I saw that our tank was upside down and blown open. Where I had been standing, there was a hole at least six feet deep. I was lying in a muddy tank tread and could feel slime all over my body. I thought my body had been ripped open and I was dying. My glasses were hanging on one ear, but I didn't have a scratch. Our tank happened to land right on its top. The guys in it were all battered up, but they lived. It was obvious that my guides were protecting me. It was the only possible answer.

Another time, we ran into a German Tiger tank during the Battle of the Bulge. We were totally exposed. We were dead meat. I heard my guides tell me to tell everybody inside not to move, which I did. The Tiger tank came right up to within eight or ten feet of us and stopped. A German officer came out of the tank and looked around. I was the gunner, so I was level with the German officer's face. I was looking right in his blue eyes, but he looked right through me. If he had seen me, I would have started pulling triggers, but we never would have survived. The other guys with me had all lain down and weren't making a sound, so they didn't know what was happening. When the German tank left, a guy we called Chief got up, looked around, and said, "We're in real trouble, we blew a track." He stepped outside and said, "Man, I didn't see those big tracks there before. That must have been a Tiger tank. God, it was lucky it didn't come while we were stuck here."

Around 1949, I was working as an engineer on the All-American Canal in the California desert. We were given notice that the project I was working on—expanding the water grid system to farmland and valleys in southern California—had lost its funding and would be shut down. I was worried about my job ending and what I was going to do next. On my way home, I stopped for a beer at a little bar on the edge of town. I sat down next to a guy at the end of the bar. The bartender was at the other end of the counter, and there was nobody else in the place. I ordered my beer, and this guy and I started talking. I told him about losing my job, and he said that in Alaska, I could make a lot more money for the same work. That got me real interested. We kept talking and pretty soon he sold me on going to Alaska. In fact, I went straight home and told my wife about it. I thought of some more questions for him, so I ran back to the bar to see if I could catch him, because he said he was just passing through town. When I got there, nobody but the bartender was there. I said, "Did you see which way that guy went?"

The bartender said, "What are you talking about?"

I said, "You know, the guy I was sitting next to at the bar."

He looked at me like I was crazy and said, "Sorry, buddy, but there was nobody sitting next to you at the bar." When I pressed him, he said I had been talking to myself, like there was somebody sitting next to me. "Frankly," he said, "I stayed at my end of the bar because you were acting kind of funny." That's when I realized the stranger had been a master from the other side.

When I asked my guides about it, they told me it was time for me to go to Alaska and that I needed to be gone by next week. I argued with them a bit but finally decided to follow their advice.

The last thing they said was, "It's imperative that you get your release from the National Guard before next week." That made sense because you're not supposed to leave the state without resigning from the National Guard or getting a transfer. I immediately called a captain who lived close by and asked if he could get me a discharge right away. He tried to talk me out of it, but I said, "No, I'm leaving the state next weekend, so I've gotta have this done right away." He said he'd work it out, and four days later he showed up with my discharge.

That was on a Thursday, and I was leaving on Saturday for Alaska. On Saturday morning, the captain showed up and said, "I need that discharge back."

I said, "Well, I'm not giving it back because I'm leaving in a few hours." He actually started to tear up. I said, "Gee, what the hell's the matter?"

He said, "We've been ordered to Korea. We're going to be out of here before the end of next week, and you're the only one with combat experience in our company. We really need you."

"Well," I said, "you're not getting me. I'm out. I've already done my stint overseas."

He tried hard to talk me out of leaving. He said, "We're not going to survive this without you, without somebody who knows what they're doing. I need your support."

As it turned out, I went to Alaska and that outfit was literally wiped out in Korea. Soon after they got there, they got into a fire-fight and most, if not all of them, were killed or captured. It was another case of my guides getting me out of danger and getting me someplace secure so I could continue to do the work I was meant to do.

4

KATHRYN HARWIG

Harwig's books include The Intuitive Advantage, Your Life in the Palm of Your Hand, *and* The Angel in the Big Pink Hat. *Harwig, who speaks and holds seminars on intuition and life after death, is a frequent presenter at retreats and conferences. She is a regular monthly guest on WCCO radio in Minneapolis, Minnesota. For more information, visit www.harwig.com.*

I 've been intuitive since I was a little girl. When I was three, I could tell people about their lives just by looking at their hands. The problem was, I grew up in a fundamentalist Christian family in a small Minnesota town. At first, my abilities were considered kind of cute, but that attitude changed dramatically as I got older. My mother was fascinated because I could predict future events, but she would also get very frightened—she would go so far as to buy Ouija boards and then burn them after they were used because paranormal abilities were considered evil.

Considering that I also had severe asthma and couldn't play and run with the other kids, I had a very abnormal childhood. What I wanted more than anything else was simply to be normal. So when I went away to college, I went out of my way to be an average person: I got married, bought a house in the suburbs, and joined a traditional church. I continued to read about spirituality, but I was careful to avoid any outward appearance of mysticism. I got a job as a probation officer and ultimately decided to go to law school because I figured there was nothing more normal and respectable than being a lawyer. My husband and I worked full time during the day and went to law school together on evenings and weekends. It was a grueling three and a half years.

One Sunday night during dinner, six weeks before I finished law school, I suddenly felt an intense pain in my chest. Minutes later, I was screaming in agony, and my husband rushed me to the emergency room. After a quick exam, an intern said I had an obstruction in my esophagus; he had me drink barium so an x-ray could be taken. I immediately went into a tailspin. What we later found out was that a hole had been ripped open in my esophagus, and the barium had flowed out of that hole and into my chest cavity. Unaware of what had happened, I was admitted to the hospital to wait for a specialist to examine me the next morning.

Overnight, the barium hardened throughout my chest cavity, which caused excruciating pain. When morning came, I had blown up like a balloon and was barely conscious. The specialist took one look at me and turned green—he knew there was something a great deal worse going on than a simple obstruction. A nurse wheeled me into a tiny little closet area and told me to wait there. I didn't know it, but the specialist was in a panic, rushing around consulting with other doctors.

Slouched in the wheelchair, I felt myself leave my body. Just like that, I was floating near the ceiling, looking down at myself. I had no attachment whatsoever to my physical body. I remember thinking, completely dispassionately, *Well, if they don't do something very quickly, it's going to die*. It was as if I was looking at a pair of socks on the floor and had to decide whether to wash them or throw them away. In that state, I traveled to the room where doctors were consulting about me. They were terrified, not only about my condition but also about malpractice issues. I later verified much of that conversation with one of the doctors who was there.

The next thing I remember is waking up. Emergency chest surgery had managed to save my life, although I was extremely ill for another five years because of the damage to my heart, lungs, pancreas, and other organs. I was told my life expectancy was five to ten years. That was twenty-five years ago. I still have a lot of pain, but I learned some self-hypnosis techniques that control it pretty well.

That ordeal turned my life upside down. Before I went in to the hospital, I was about to finish law school in the top 10 percent of my class. I was going to get a job with a big law firm, make a lot of money, and have all the things that society values. But after I got out of the hospital, none of that mattered. My physical body and material objects meant nothing to me anymore. I did practice law for a while but never did go to a big firm. I set up my own small shop, but as time passed, I couldn't shake the feeling that I was supposed to be doing something else.

After much turmoil, I finally came to the realization that if nothing material really mattered, then the only important things were spiritual matters. That was when I began re-exploring the gifts I had been given in childhood and how I could use them to help people.

To this day, whenever I think about that morning in the hospital when I was looking down at my body slumped in a wheelchair, it reminds me that we can slip out of our skins as easily as we can slip out of our clothes—and that's about how much our bodies actually mean to us. I'm still attached to my physical body and material possessions, of course, but I'm keenly aware of how ephemeral they are—they can easily slip right through our hands. I do my best to keep my attention focused on what truly matters.

5

JAMES VAN PRAAGH

Van Praagh, one of the world's best-known spiritual mediums, bridges the gap between the living and dead by providing evidential proof of life after death via detailed messages from those who have passed on. The first of his five books, Talking to Heaven, *served as the inspiration for the 2002 CBS miniseries,* Living with the Dead, *starring Ted Danson. That miniseries, in turn, inspired* Ghost Whisperer, *a weekly CBS drama starring Jennifer Love Hewitt and co-executive produced by Van Praagh. His daytime talk show,* Beyond with James Van Praagh, *aired in the United States during the 2002–2003 season and is still being shown throughout the world. For more information, visit www.vanpraagh.com.*

One of my earliest encounters with the spiritual realm was when I was in my early twenties and my life was saved by spirit. This was long before I started doing the work I do now.

It was past midnight on a Saturday night when I left a party at a friend's house. I was driving an old car—I think it was a 1967 Impala—because I had just moved to Los Angeles and I had no money. The gas gauge on the dashboard didn't work, so I had to go by mileage to estimate how much gas I had left. Sure enough, on my way home at one in the morning, I ran out of gas. Thank God it was at a busy intersection in Hollywood and there was a gas station right on the corner. I walked over to the station, and they filled up a gas can for me.

Like a lot of older cars, the gas tank was under the license plate, so I went around to the back of the car and kneeled down to open it. That's when I found out that the gas can they had given me was leaking. Still, I was trying to make it work when, suddenly, I noticed an older man with snow-white hair standing to my right. I remember that he had very sweet eyes. He said, "You must go back to the service station and get another gas can right away." I didn't even question him. I don't know why. I guess I was just in a really weird state because I had run out of gas in the middle of a busy intersection at one in the morning on a Saturday night in Hollywood.

So I got up and walked back over to the service station to get a new gas can. As I was knocking on the window, I heard a loud bang. I looked back and watched in shock as my car rolled down the street, onto a sidewalk, and into a lamppost. A car had plowed into mine from behind. I looked for the old man, but he was nowhere to be found, even though only a half a minute had passed. I was so shaken that it didn't dawn on me until the next morning that I could have easily been killed. If it wasn't for that man, I would've been bent over putting gas in my tank, and that car would've driven right into me. Looking back, I know he was an angel. I have no doubt about it.

6

DOREEN VIRTUE, Ph.D.

Virtue, a spiritual clairvoyant, holds B.A., M.A., and Ph.D. degrees in counseling psychology. She is the author of twenty-two books on mind-body-spirit issues, including Healing with the Angels, Divine Guidance, *and* Eating in the Light. *She is the founder and former director of WomanKind Psychiatric Hospital at Cumberland Hall Hospital in Nashville, Tennessee. For more information, visit* www.angeltherapy.com.

Throughout my career, I had gotten in the habit of ignoring my divine guidance because my angels had been hounding me to quit my job as a psychotherapist and to teach people about spiritual healing instead. There was no way I was going to do that! I was a published author and a well-respected psychotherapist. If I were to start talking about things like angels and life after death, I would lose everything!

I stopped arguing with my angels on July 15, 1995, the day that ignoring their advice almost cost me my life. I was getting ready to go to an appointment in Anaheim, California, from my house in Newport Beach. I was alone in my bedroom getting dressed when I heard a male voice very clearly say, "You better put the top up on your car or it's going to be stolen." I understood what the voice meant because I had a cute little BMW 325i; I kept the top down because the motor which elevated the top was broken. The voice repeated the warning three more times, but I kept arguing with it. I said I couldn't get the top up, and besides, I was in such a hurry to get to my appointment that I didn't have time to deal with it.

When I pulled into the parking lot near my appointment an hour later, I was jumped by two armed men who demanded my car keys and my purse. It was an entirely different scenario than I had imagined—I thought that if my car were going to be stolen, it would be while I was in the building. Fortunately, my angel hadn't abandoned me. He told me, "Scream with all your might," and this time I listened to him. I didn't even know I had it in me to scream so loud, but that's exactly what I did. My scream attracted the attention of people in the building, and a woman in the parking lot started leaning on her horn. The eyes of the carjacker closest to me got as big as saucers, and they both ran away.

After that incident, so many changes began occurring in my life both personally and professionally. First of all, I was so shocked about the angel's prescience that I began doing a great deal of research, including interviewing people who had also been warned by angels. My research showed me that these experiences weren't paranormal at all. They were normal and very common; it's just that people weren't talking about them.

When I asked the angels what I should do next, they told me to stop doing psychotherapy and to do angel therapy instead. They also told me to stop charging for my services! I protested because I didn't know how I would pay my bills, but they just told me not to worry about it. Well, right away, one speaking engagement after another started rolling in. I was also told to write a book consisting of messages from the angels, so I emailed my publisher and told him I wanted to write a book called *Angel Therapy*. I didn't tell him what it was about because I didn't know myself! He wrote me back within an hour and said, "Yes, we'll publish that book." I had been very concerned about having enough money coming in, but there was never even a hiccup with my finances.

Now it's clear to me that when you follow your divine guidance, you'll probably find yourself living by the seat of your pants. But the payoff is that your life becomes enriched with wonderfully vivid colors, both metaphorically and literally. I've never had such joy and so much love and abundance and meaning in my life. I wake up in the morning excited about the kind of work I do. It's been a real miracle all the way around.

7

LARRY DOSSEY, M.D.

Dr. Dossey's ten books include The Extraordinary Healing Power of Ordinary Things, Reinventing Medicine, *and* Healing Words. *Dr. Dossey, the executive editor of* Explore: The Journal of Science and Healing, *a peer-reviewed, bimonthly publication, has become an internationally influential advocate of the mind's role in health and the role of spirituality in healthcare. For more information, visit www.dosseydossey.com and www.explorejournal.com.*

The most important aspect of my spiritual life is a sense of oneness with the divine. It permeates my life and manifests as a sense of oneness and unity with other people.

A lot of people believe that unless they have some sort of incredible, life-changing, sudden epiphany, their spiritual journey is not valid or genuine. We have to guard against that. The spiritual path is extraordinarily varied, and it comes in many flavors. One of the things I would want to suggest to folks is that it's the depth and the endurance that really matter, not the pyrotechnics, the fireworks that one may experience from time to time.

A fundamental part of my spiritual development has involved science, most dramatically in the study of distance healing and intercessory prayer, which I've written about extensively. I consider the scientific studies supporting the power of prayer to be evidence of the unity that the great mystics have described throughout history.

My research has convinced me that we are all connected at some very deep level, across space and time, in ways that we scarcely perceive in waking consciousness. There seems to be a benevolent, quite wonderful side to the universe; otherwise, healing through thought and intention and prayer could not be expected to take place.

Although there have been no incredible moments in my life that one would call epiphanies, I've had experiences of what I call nonlocal mind (akin to collective consciousness) uniting me with my patients through dreams. These dreams, which generally occurred the night before I was to see the patient involved, were extremely vivid and full of clinical facts.

For example, during my first year of practice as an internist in a Dallas hospital, I dreamt about Justin, the four-year-old son of a colleague. I had met this child only a few times and certainly didn't know him well. In the dream, he was stretched out on an examination table and one of his parents was trying to comfort him. There was some sort of medical technician trying to do something to his head, but Justin would have none of it; he was going berserk. Finally, the medical technician threw up her hands and said, "I give up; I quit!" and walked away. The dream was so vivid and disturbing that I almost woke my wife up to tell her about it.

Later that day at lunch, I was having a sandwich in the cafeteria with Justin's father. Suddenly, his wife approached us carrying their little boy, who was crying. She told her husband she had just come from the EEG (electroencephalography) lab where a technician had been trying to obtain a brain-wave tracing. But Justin had gone berserk and would not cooperate. It was such a chaotic fiasco that the technician, who had never before been thwarted in her efforts to obtain an EEG tracing on a child, had finally given up and abandoned the procedure. I was speechless because I had dreamt this event in almost photographic detail the night before.

I later went to my colleague's office and said, "Look, we need to talk. Is there any way that I could have known that your child was scheduled for an EEG today?"

He said, "Don't be silly, of course not. No one knew except my wife and I and the neurologist." He said that Justin had developed a fever the day before and had had a brief seizure, so his parents had made an appointment for a quick consultation.

When I told him about my dream, he was extremely disturbed and wanted to hear no more of it. He knew in an instant, as did I, that if we took this dream seriously, we would have to revise our idea of reality, of the very nature of how the world worked. It took me years to revisit that experience, which I finally did in the book *Reinventing Medicine*.

8

WAYNE W. DYER, Ph.D.

Dyer, affectionately called the "Father of Motivation" by his legion of fans, is one of the most widely known and respected people in the field of self-empowerment. He became a well-known author with his bestselling book Your Erroneous Zones *and has gone on to write many other self-help classics, including* Manifest Your Destiny, There's a Spiritual Solution to Every Problem, *and* 10 Secrets for Success and Inner Peace. *For more information, visit www.drwaynedyer.com.*

In October 2000, I led a tour group of twenty-five or thirty people to the French town of Lourdes, where the Virgin Mary had appeared repeatedly to Bernadette Soubirous, a local fourteen-year-old girl, almost 150 years ago. The "magic water" in the grotto there had healed thousands of people over the years, and as many as twenty thousand people had come from all over the world just to be in this beautiful place—about three thousand of them in wheelchairs or on stretchers. At night there was a procession, and all the people gathered by the grotto where the Virgin Mary had appeared to Saint Bernadette. Nobody had organized anything, and nobody told anybody what to do. The song "Ave Maria" was playing in five different languages throughout the entire city, everyone had candles, and we all just showed up and quietly marched. It was one of the most peaceful, magical, and beautiful experiences I've ever had in my life; it lasted about two hours, and I didn't want it to end.

The next day, we flew to Paris and turned on the TV for the first time in several weeks. All the news coverage showed Israelis and Palestinians throwing rocks at each other on the West Bank, and I thought to myself that what we had experienced in Lourdes was a much greater story. That beautiful procession happens every single night between April and October of every year, and all the people there come to celebrate peace and love and forgiveness and healing. And what gets all the attention on the news? A few hundred people throwing rocks at each other.

Our next stop was Assisi, Italy, the birthplace of Francesco Bernadone, who was better known as Saint Francis of Assisi. I had been lecturing to the group about Saint Francis, and we had had many discussions about the power of his words and his life. Saint Francis was the first person to experience the stigmata—the wounds of Christ. In fact, many feel that he *was* Christ, reincarnated thirteen centuries later. It's been said that his personal energy was so powerful that anyone who walked near him would automatically be healed. The Hindu author Patanjali once said, "When you become steadfast in your abstention of thoughts of harm directed toward others, all living creatures will cease to feel enmity in your presence." Saint Francis personified that peaceful and reverential approach to life, and I look to him as a model for what I aspire to be in my own life.

We then visited a castle in San Damiano just outside of Assisi—the home of the convent that Saint Francis had set up for Saint Clare, the first female admitted into the Franciscan order. Our plan was to walk up to the third level to see the place where Saint Clare had died. A young man named John Graybill was the first one up the stairs, and I was right behind him. John was twenty-two years old and weighed nearly two hundred pounds with his leg braces on, which he wore because, as he said, his body—not he—had muscular dystrophy. When we got up eight or nine steps, the staircase started to narrow and John realized to his dismay that he couldn't go any farther—he couldn't extend his legs to the left or to the right, which is the only way he could manage to climb a flight of stairs. He turned to me and said, "I don't know what I'm going to do. I can't go back down the steps because of all the people in line, and I can't go up because I can't move my legs."

I immediately said, "Why don't you get on my back and I'll carry you?"

But I had forgotten a couple of things—I forgot that I was sixty years old, and I also forgot that I had serious ligament and cartilage damage in my knees that required surgery. (I had run eight miles a day, every day, for twenty-two years and had also played a lot of tennis, so for the last several years I had been forced to wear a brace while doing those activities.) After going up just a couple of steps with John on my back, I suddenly felt my knees starting to crumble. At that very moment, I had a vision of Saint Francis, and suddenly my knees went from crumbling to becoming straight and erect and strong. I also had an incredible burst of energy like I've never had before in my entire life. I didn't just walk up the rest of the stairs, I *ran* up the last two and a half flights with John on my back!

When I got to the top, I wasn't even winded. My wife was incredulous. She said, "How could you have carried him up like that? You were running but you still have all of this energy!" Everyone was shocked over what I had just done, including me. I went out on the balcony, put my hands together in prayer, and gave thanks to Saint Francis for what seemed like a miraculous healing. Unbeknownst to me, a woman named Pat Eagan who was on the trip with us snapped a photo of me in that position. When she sent the photo to me, I was so struck by it that I sent it off to my publisher—and they decided to use it on the cover of the book I had just written, *There's a Spiritual Solution to Every Problem*. The experience affected me so much that when I got back to America, I reformulated the book so that the last seven chapters were each titled after a line in Saint Francis's famous prayer:

The Prayer of Saint Francis of Assisi

Lord, make me an instrument of your peace;
where there is hatred, let me sow love;
where there is injury, pardon;
where there is doubt, faith;
where there is despair, hope;
where there is darkness, light;
where there is sadness, joy.

O Divine Master, grant that I may not so much seek
to be consoled as to console;
to be understood as to understand;
to be loved as to love.

For it is in giving that we receive;
it is in pardoning that we are pardoned;
and it is in dying that we are born to eternal life.

That run up the stairs with John on my back was one of the most miraculous and life-changing events in my life. It will be seven years this October and my knees are completely healed— I no longer have to wear braces to play tennis or to run. It's clear to me that the divinely inspired energy of Saint Francis is still at work today in that ancient castle.

9

TOM GEGAX

Gegax is a sought-after business consultant and speaker. His book,
The Big Book of Small Business: You Don't Have to Run Your
Business by the Seat of Your Pants, *is a comprehensive guide that
combines hard-nosed accountability and efficiency (profits first)
with a caring approach (people first) in one practical package that
honors both. Gegax is cofounder and chairman emeritus of Tires
Plus, the largest independent tire store chain in the country. For
more information, visit www.gegax.com.*

I n 1989, I thought my life was working pretty well. Then, within a
six-month period, I was diagnosed with cancer, my twenty-five-
year marriage ended, and my chief financial officer came into my
office and said, "Tom, the bank account is a million dollars short
and our credit line is exhausted. What are we going to do?" So, just
like that, the three major areas of my life—my health, my love relationship, and my career—were in shambles. And I was hit with the
stark reality that not only had my life *not* been working but that I
had played a major role in causing it all to come tumbling down.

That was when I began seeking a different way of being in the
world. I knew I had to remake myself and create mutually fulfilling relationships in all areas of my life in order to be truly happy.
It was a long, painful process, but by exploring healthier lifestyles
and making better choices, I was eventually able to reclaim my
health, find a wonderful woman to share my life with, and build
my business into an industry leader.

Three years after that triple trauma, I took a meditative trip to the Greek islands with the express purpose of getting more in touch with myself, something I wasn't able to do amidst the busyness of everyday life. I had heard the Greeks had the worst phone system in the world, so I decided to go there for a retreat. I did a little sightseeing, but most of my time was spent meditating day and night in my room. There was no schedule for when I would eat or sleep. I wanted to get lost, not in thought, but in just being.

Remember in the movie *Cocoon* when two people were across the pool from each other but were having virtually orgasmic, bliss-like experiences? That's how I felt. I was able to get in trance-like states that were incredible, just sitting there meditating, not thinking about any of life's challenges, feeling a deep sense of connection with everything. It was a unique state of feeling grounded yet being one with the universe. I had meditated before but had never been in such a deep state.

One night, after a particularly blissful, meditative day, I woke up at 3 AM. On the pillow next to me was a bright, glowing treasure chest. I was wide awake; this chest was definitely not a figment of my imagination. I stared at it for ten or fifteen seconds and finally thought, *I've gotta try to touch this thing.* As my hand drew closer to the chest, it slowly dissipated until it was gone. I got right up and wrote it all down, in case I would try to fool myself the next morning into thinking it hadn't happened. The meaning of it was very clear to me—that if you take more time to meditate and go within, the treasures are immense.

For another week, until I flew back home, everything seemed so bright and magical. It was like I was living in a fantasyland. My senses were so heightened and powerful, and I was experiencing life to a greater degree than I ever had before. I'd love to say, yes, I visit that space all the time, but even though I've gone on a few more retreats since then, I have not yet been able to duplicate that experience.

10

ANDREW HARVEY

Harvey, an author, teacher, and mystical scholar, has written and edited more than thirty books. His own works include Son of Man: The Mystical Path to Christ; The Sun at Midnight: A Memoir of the Dark Night; *and* A Walk with Four Spiritual Guides: Krishna, Buddha, Jesus, and Ramakrishna. *His DVD,* Sacred Activism, *is available at www.hartleyfoundation.org. For more information, visit www.andrewharvey.net.*

In 1997, my mother sent me a fax from Coimbatore in southern India, where I was born, saying that my father was dying and that I should get there as quickly as possible. I was living in San Francisco at the time. I managed to get a visa within two days and got to his bedside in the next week.

What followed was the most beautiful week of my life because my father and I were able to communicate at a level and depth and true spiritual height that we had never managed before. All our political and personal differences were drowned in great sweetness and tender communication. And I realized how finely and absolutely he had always loved me and how much he had always held me in his heart. This was in itself a huge healing. But another healing on an even larger scale was going to take place.

During our time together, my father and I did not talk about anything that had ever happened between us. What we talked about was Jesus. My father spoke out of the depth of his passionate and simple faith in Jesus. Now that he was facing death, he was speaking inwardly to Jesus in Gethsemane—because, as he said, Jesus knows everything about terrors of the heart, and He accompanies us in whatever anguish and loneliness we go into.

"So now I am facing death as He faced it in the garden of Gethsemane," my father said. "I'm speaking to him as if He were in the garden, so that He can help me."

I was deeply moved by my father's faith and by the simplicity and purity and nobility of it. And I understood that my father's great qualities as a human being—courtesy, humility, generosity, tolerance—had been rooted in a lifelong spiritual friendship with the Christ. Many times as we spoke, I felt in the room the presence of an extraordinary power that enfolded us in wings of light. And he felt it too.

On his deathbed, I was able to teach my father a practice that I had learned from the Tibetan masters on how to visualize the Divine Beloved in whatever form you love Him or Her so that you could enter into total relationship with the divine. One of the greatest joys of my life is that, before he died, he said to my mother that he had practiced this visualization and that he had indeed seen the living Christ.

I had arrived in Coimbatore on a Tuesday. That Sunday, I went to services at a Catholic church called The Church of Christ the King. A small, plump Indian priest gave an utterly simple and heartbreaking sermon about how Christ is the mystical king of reality—not only because of the miracles that Jesus did, or the enormous influence that He has had, but because of Jesus' abandoned service to all beings out of complete compassion and complete and final love.

These words absolutely pierced my soul. I had been utterly flayed by my closeness to my father's dying and had been completely opened by the bliss and heartbreak that passed between us. I heard the priest's words as if they were spoken to me directly to wake me up to the essence of the spiritual path—which is, I believe, service in all its forms in the spirit of absolute, tender compassion to all beings.

When the priest finished talking and sat down, I looked up at the statue of the resurrected Christ at the end of the church. To my absolute awe and astonishment, it became alive and began to emit radiant golden light. I knew beyond a shadow of any doubt that the living resurrected Christ was appearing to me and radiating toward me, burning an infinite passion. My whole being trembled and blazed in the exquisite, terrible, fierce, glorious force of intense, ecstatic passion flowing from Him to me. As this force entered me, it seemed to hack my chest open and split open my heart so that from the depths of my heart a smaller answering force started to radiate back to the great force emanating from the Christ.

And in those sacred moments, I understood the truth of what the great mystics of divine love of all traditions have been trying to teach us—that lover, beloved, and love are one, and that this oneness in the burning, tender communion of divine love is the absolute and final reality of the universe.

I was standing next to my brother, who is a banker, so I had to control myself. But tears of rapture and gratitude and infinite joy poured from my eyes. And I felt that one period of my life had ended and a whole new period was beginning. I had been in a savage and frightening dark night of the soul for many years, undergoing a stripping and searing and burning of all of my ideas and agendas. This supreme experience signaled to me the dawn of my own inmost, divine identity. I knew from a study of Christian mystical literature that experiences of the risen Christ such as this very often signaled the end of the dark night and the beginning of consciousness of divine identity.

The experience did not end with my vision, however. As I stumbled out of church into the blazing noon of an Indian morning,

I saw a young man, without arms or legs, in a filthy shirt, squatting miserably and desolately in a puddle. He was one of the most beautiful human beings I had ever seen, with a face absolutely purified by extreme pain and extreme suffering. As I helped him out of the puddle, I realized that just as I had seen the living Christ in the statue, now I was seeing Him in this desperate being before me. And as I gazed into the eyes of the broken Christ, I heard a thunderous voice within me say

You have been playing with light for years now and have been using the mystical experiences that the divine has given you for your own satisfaction, your own career, and your own self-aggrandizement. You must stop this because the only purpose of mystical awakening is to make you a servant of divine love in the world and help you to dedicate all of your thoughts, emotions, actions, and resources to the dissolution of those circumstances that create the torment, misery, loneliness, dejection, and desolation that you see before you. In this tormented world, threatened by extinction, it is time you realize, Andrew, that you must turn from every form of narcissism and self-absorption. It is time for you to dedicate your entire work to bringing about the revolution of Christ consciousness in the world, so that human beings can transform themselves and the conditions they create, and so that nature can be preserved, because the world is in extreme and potentially terminal danger.

These words—and of course I am paraphrasing them and putting them into language because they came to me in great blocks of fierce emotion—have been the guiding force behind all the work that I have done in these last years. My experience in the church has never died in me, and I don't believe it will ever die in me. In every moment of every day, I feel the presence of that flame of divine passion in the core of my heart. And I know that the one hope for humanity is to take up the challenge of the living Christ—to put divine love and divine compassion into radical transformative action on every level and in every arena of the world so as to transform the world before the destructive power of humanity utterly and completely devastates it.

This sacred activism, which is how I express my vision of the Christ, is for me a fusion of the deepest level of mystical practice of stamina, strength, passion, peace, and clarity with focused, wise, nonviolent, radical action in the real world. I know that this work of sacred activism is the work of the Christ consciousness and that this work is crucial for the preservation of the planet. I believe that everyone who is mystically awake and who is awake to the terrible destruction that is now happening in the world will be summoned by the divine to this fusion of inner practice with radical action that I was summoned to on that November day in Coimbatore.

This revelation came to me in terms of the Christ because of my Christian background, but I know it is coming to millions of people all over the world in terms of their own religious traditions or symbols. And when it comes, it comes as it did to me, in a blaze of infinite joy and peace and rapture—and in a blaze of agonized compassion. This fusion of rapture and agonized compassion is the hallmark of what is known in the mystical traditions as the sacred heart, the heart center, the heart truth.

This experience has given me a tremendous faith in the next stage of human evolution. It was the beginning of a birth—a birth of the presence of the divine inside my heart and mind and body. I know that this birth is not mine alone but is happening in the middle of the chaos and the madness of our time—and partly through that chaos—all over the planet. And it is this birth—this birth of a new, divine human that has a total focus on justice and on transformative sacred action —that offers the great hope for the future.

It is this birth, in fact, that is the secret meaning of the apocalyptic situation we are now going through. It signals that what we are dealing with is potentially not the end of everything but the beginning of a new divine humanity. And this apocalyptic situation is, in fact, the birth canal—the terrible, amazing birth canal—of a new divine human being capable of cocreating, in and under the divine, a holy new world.

11

CAROLINE MYSS

Myss, a renowned medical intuitive who lectures all over the world on the untapped potential of the human spirit, is the author of four New York Times *bestsellers:* Anatomy of the Spirit, Why People Don't Heal and How They Can, Sacred Contracts, *and her latest effort,* Entering the Castle. *For more information, visit www.myss.com.*

I had gradually become aware of Sai Baba (an avatar born in India in 1926) over the last decade or so because stories about him kept surfacing. I'd find out that friends of mine were devotees. So I was curious about him. Of course, when I saw what he looked like, I thought, *You've got to be kidding.* First of all, the very idea that I would consider devotion first to a human being—I could not process that; that didn't work in my personal theology. Number two, I couldn't seem to get worked up about Hinduism. So we've got a human being *and* a Hindu. And then someone who wears his hair like that! So on all burners, you have somebody who's not making a lot of sense to me. And that makes my devotion all the more amazing because I am not easily seduced. I truly am not. But over the years—how can I say this?—our paths have crossed in some pretty amazing ways. So I would occasionally say a silent prayer like, *Baba, if you can hear me, if you're out there, I could use your help.* And then I would add as an aside, *Yo, Jesus, Mary, and anyone else up there on the Christian team, if I'm screwing up here, it's not from a lack of faith, it's that I'm just visiting. Let's not make this a big, huge deal, okay?*

So am I superstitious? Yes. I am respectfully, spiritually super-stitious. I have too much Catholic in me to not pay attention to my Catholic history and too much devotion to Jesus, Mary, and the Christian mystic teachings. I also am dominantly a mono-theist. So turning my devotion to Baba was potentially a real crisis for me. I mean, who is this man and why am I so drawn to him? That was very, very difficult for me and still is. At the end of the day, what I usually do is run away and go back to *there is only one God in many forms*, and that's the end of that.

The first time I called on Sai Baba was more than ten years ago during a health scare I had when I was in northern Scotland. You have to understand that I'm in the middle of nowhere and nobody but my friends know I'm there. I said, *Baba, I don't even know why I'm praying to you. But if you're there and if you're lis-tening, I think I'd like some of that vibhuti* (the holy ash used in religious worship that Sai Baba reportedly materializes at will). Now why would I ask for vibhuti? I've never asked for that in my life. Holy water, yeah. Holy oil, uh-huh. Holy ash, no. "Ash" to me is Ash Wednesday. Ash has its own sacred place in the Christian tradition. But in India, ash is *the* sacred element.

So the next day—the very next day!—this little tube the size of a 35mm film canister arrives filled with vibhuti with a note that reads, "To Caroline Myss, from Sai Baba." This was within twelve hours of my prayer, and I'm up where Christ lost his shoe in the Highlands of Scotland! The package had come via someone I had met many years earlier who had come to three of my lectures in Copenhagen. I didn't even know this man! Do you know how many thousands of people I meet? Do you think I would give this man my address, much less my social schedule, plus call him up and tell him I'm going to see a few friends in northern Scotland in case he needs to reach me? Do you understand how ridiculous that is? That's why getting that package impressed me so much. I mean, if I had gotten a call from a very close friend who said, "Hey, I just got you some vibhuti," that would have been impressive enough. But to actually have a package arrive, delivered by someone I didn't even know, was way beyond impressive. And where did he mail it? To where I was visiting friends in a remote part of Scotland! A stalker couldn't do a better job!

From that point on, Baba had my attention. And I started to experience connections with him on a fairly regular basis. For example, when my older brother Joe was critically ill and my younger brother Eddie was dealing with some very stressful circumstances, my mother said to me, "Can't you do something? Can't you write Sai Baba?"

I said, "What do you think I should do, Mom? Address an envelope to Sai Baba care of India? I have no idea where he lives." I woke up the next morning to find that his address had been faxed to me from somebody in Australia!

After the container of vibhuti had shown up in Scotland, I took it with me wherever I traveled. It was precious to me. It was like having my own altar, a direct phone line to this mysterious being who always knew where I was. Not long after, I was doing a workshop with Norm Shealy at Norm's farm. I made the mistake of telling this group of twenty-eight people about the vibhuti and everybody was like, "I want some, I want some." It was just too much for me. I thought, *Go away! How dare you ask for this? How dare you?* But then it occurred to me that there was something I needed to learn from this. So I opened up the canister and told people to just touch it a little bit. One man stuck his finger in all the way to the bottom and I said, "Do you understand what I just said to you? Why did you do that? This ash is sacred to me. What is it with you people having to be so greedy?" I mean, I leveled him. He came up to me later and apologized. On top of that, a woman in the group came up and said to me, "My aunt is dying; she's a devotee of Sai Baba. Can I take some to her?" And I thought, *Can you take some to her? I'm already halfway out of it!* Well, her aunt had never been to India so I put a little vibhuti in a Kleenex for her. But I was raging. I was raging at my own stupidity that I'd just shared something so precious so carelessly. I put the lid back on the container and it's never gone out with me again. It's upstairs in my room and that's where it's going to stay. Well, about six weeks after that workshop, I got a letter. I still don't know who it was from. There was no postmark. It was filled with seven packages of vibhuti and a note that read, "These are from Baba. He says thank you."

Then, in the summer of 1999, I was tested for lupus. I was really terrified because it's an ugly disease and I had lost my best friend to it. I was told I would have to wait at least a week for the results. On the day of the test, I prayed to Sai Baba. And even though I still didn't really know much about him, I prayed, *I am going to come to India to see you. And if I'm going because I'm sick, I'm going to count on you to help me. And if I'm going because I'm not sick, it'll be through gratitude.* The very next day, I received a call that the blood test was negative.

Soon after, I flew to India and spent five days at Sai Baba's ashram. Five days is nothing; many people go there for five *months*. When I first saw the ashram, it blew me away because it was so not like the beautiful Catholic monasteries and convents I was used to. It was small, concrete, and just visually awful. There were thousands of people crowded outside. It was intensely hot, and it was very uncomfortable.

You had to wait six hours in the blazing hot sun in order to go in and watch Baba come in for twenty minutes. When people were allowed to go into the mandir, the huge open temple, they would practically kill each other to get the best seat in the house. And the smell! I am such a stickler for high-voltage hygiene that it was very difficult for me. There was a sense of brutality and horribleness to it all. I was just shocked.

Well, I'm sitting there in this mass of humanity, and somebody comes up to me and tells me I'm wanted at the guest office. And I'm thinking, *How did they find me out of thousands and thousands of people and how did they even know I was here?* I find my way to the office and two people I've never seen before give me some kind of ribbon and tell me I've been awarded VIP status because Baba wants me to sit in the front. How and why that happened, I have no idea. Nobody knew I was there or that I was an American writer—nobody over there cares about who you are.

When Baba comes to darshan, which is his twice-daily appearance in the mandir, he walks around at ground level and people desperately thrust personal letters toward him. Every so often, he'll take a letter, which I could tell was a really big deal for people. So what the heck, I thought I'd write a letter too. The next day, he walked past me, turned around, came back, and asked for my letter. After the darshan, people were streaming up and kissing the ground in front of where Baba had stood when he had asked for my letter. I was told that it was out of character for Baba to stop and actually ask for someone's letter. I mean, it was really a big deal for these people. I didn't expect or receive any response from giving Baba the letter. It was more like an act of faith.

So where do I stand today? I still don't have any answers, but Baba's presence in my life has become a constant. And I find that very, very comforting.

12

TRENT TUCKER

Tucker, who still ranks as one of the top ten three-point shooters in NBA history, played for the New York Knicks, San Antonio Spurs, and Chicago Bulls in an eleven-year career, winning a world championship with the Bulls in 1993. A graduate of the University of Minnesota, Tucker is currently a broadcast analyst for a Minneapolis sports-talk radio station. A longtime community activist, he founded the Trent Tucker Non-Profit Organization to empower youth to make positive choices, elevate their self-respect, and develop a positive vision for the future. For more information, visit www.trenttucker.org.

In 1983, my second year in the NBA with the New York Knicks, there was a month-long stretch where I wasn't playing. Players always want to play, so I was looking for an opportunity to get in the game somehow, someway. Remember, we're talking about a kid who was twenty-three years old and thought basketball meant everything.

Two veterans on the team, Louis Orr and Truck Robinson, were nice enough to give me a helping hand during that period. They helped me understand what I needed to do to keep in shape, so that when I got the call, I would be ready to go. And they enlightened me about what I needed to do in order to grow, not only as a basketball player, but as a person as well.

I'm not the most religious guy in the world, but I have a strong faith and I believe in God. You know how you hear people talk sometimes about a spirit that came and uplifted them and moved them in the right direction? Well, one night, a spirit walked into Madison Square Garden and gave me an opportunity to play basketball again.

Ray Williams, one of the guys who was playing in front of me, went down with an ankle sprain. All of a sudden, I felt something come into the Garden. I looked up and saw this spirit coming down the aisle at the opposite end of the court down by the visitors' bench behind the basket. It looked like a cloud. I knew right away that it was a higher force, a positive force, and that what was happening was very real. I could feel it remove all the tension and apprehension I was going through, and I could feel it telling me, *I'm here. I'm going to support you. You have done what you were supposed to do. It's time to go out and play now. Your time has come.*

The vision stayed for four or five minutes. I remember feeling very at ease, very calm; it was a pleasant feeling. It was unfortunate that Ray went down, but I knew that this was how my prayers were being answered. Sure enough, in the second half of that game, I went from not playing at all to starting full time. A few weeks later, when Ray had recovered, our coach, Hubie Brown, said, "Trent, I've got to go with the guy who started in front of you because he's a veteran and he's been here longer."

I said, "Hey, that's cool with me."

I was at ease and just thankful that I got a chance to help the team during that stretch. It felt good to be a contributor. I went back to the bench, but this time, I was a regular player off the bench—before Ray's injury, I hadn't been playing at all. Then we got to the playoffs, and the coach made some adjustments. He decided to put me back in the starting lineup because I was a better fit with the other guys who were starting—and he thought Ray would be a better guy coming off the bench.

But the important thing was that going through my experience gave me a whole new perspective on life. It had been a lifetime dream of mine to get to the NBA, and I thought that sitting on the bench and not playing was the end of the world. My encounter with that spirit allowed me to understand that there were more important things I could be concerned about than not playing in a basketball game. I realized that I should be thankful that I had the privilege to play at the NBA level because I was very lucky to be one of the few guys who had a chance to do that for a living. But when you're young and you want to play, you don't see those things right away.

From that point on, I could always see the bigger picture, and nothing seemed to bother me. I became a person who was at ease in whatever situation I was in. I could react to situations and talk to people differently because I had removed myself away from myself and it wasn't all about Trent Tucker anymore.

I became a thinker instead of a reactor. I learned that when you feel that a situation isn't going in the right direction, you have a better chance of dealing with it in a positive way if you sit down and think about things and put a plan together before you react—because if you react before you think, you can put yourself in a worse situation.

Today, as a forty-seven-year-old man, I can still see that spirit as clearly as I saw it back then. I thank God every day that I was able to see and feel that spirit because it changed me, broadened my horizons, and made me a better person.

13

NEALE DONALD WALSCH

Walsch is a modern-day spiritual messenger whose words are touching the world. He has written twenty-three books on spirituality and its practical application in everyday life, including the multimillion-selling, nine-book With God series: Conversations with God: Books I–III; Friendship with God; Communion with God; The New Revelations; Tomorrow's God; What God Wants; *and* Home with God in a Life That Never Ends. *Six of those books made the* New York Times *Bestseller List;* Conversations with God: Book 1 *occupied the list for more than 135 weeks. Walsch is the creator of four nonprofit organizations: The Group of 1000, Humanity's Team, the School of the New Spirituality, and the ReCreation Foundation. For more information, visit www.nealedonaldwalsch.com.*

How *Conversations with God* first came to me was the most profound experience of my life. It was a dreary morning in February 1992. Everything in my life had fallen apart—my relationship with my significant other had gone downhill, my career had reached a dead end, and even my health was deteriorating rapidly. I couldn't understand what was happening or why. I had obeyed all the rules I had been carefully taught by my parents, teachers, ministers, and various other life mentors, but I simply hadn't achieved what I thought I ought to have achieved. And so I was deeply in depression for a number of months.

I was awakened at 4:15 in the morning. I was deeply troubled, very frustrated, and very angry with God. I went to the larger part of the house and just started pacing, not knowing what to do or how to deal with these emotions I was having.

I picked up a yellow legal pad that I found on the coffee table and began writing an angry letter to God. The letter was filled with all the typical questions we ask when we have a lot of anger, such as *What does it take for me to have my life work?; What have I done to deserve a life of such continuing struggle?; Somebody tell me the rules, because I'll play if you'll just tell me the rules!*

Then I heard a voice as clearly as anything I have ever heard. It was a physical voice, there in the room. And the voice said, "Neale, do you really want answers to all of these questions, or are you just venting?" I couldn't believe it. I looked around to see if anybody was there. Nobody was, so I said to myself, *Well, I am venting, but if you've got answers, I'd sure as heck like to know what they are.* And with that, I began receiving answers to all the questions I had been asking.

I picked up the yellow legal pad again and began writing down what I was now hearing in my head. As I was writing, I began asking other questions in my mind; as I did so, I immediately received other answers. And as I wrote those answers down, I received other questions. Before I knew it, I was involved in an on-paper dialogue with God. I wouldn't have called it "God" at the time, of course. I didn't know what was happening. I just knew that I was asking the deepest questions of my life and getting answers right then and there.

It was a very moving moment. I was weeping as I wrote, weeping at the beauty and the wonder of it and also at the feeling I was having, which was a feeling of great peace and serenity inside. This went on for two and a half hours. Then the house started getting up, so I stopped, although I could've gone on forever. The same thing happened at 4:15 the next morning and again every night thereafter for two and a half or three weeks. Then it began to taper off—instead of every night, it began happening two or three times a week, then once a week. Over the period of the next year, I continued to have these experiences. The result was *Conversations with God: Book 1*, which became a publishing phenomenon and was translated into thirty-seven languages.

That initial event changed my life completely. It affected me deeply and returned me to my grandest notion about God, which is that God is utterly without judgment and is always there and willing to communicate with us and help us, if we'll only open ourselves to that possibility and that experience.

Part II

LIVING LIFE

Travelers, it is late. Life's sun is going to set.
During these brief days that you have strength,
be quick and spare no effort of your wings.
Rumi

We never know what tomorrow may bring. At any given moment, the foundation of our life may shift under our feet. A disease is diagnosed. A stranger reaches out in need. A new soul enters the world, or an old one leaves. These events and how we deal with them change our life, and more importantly, change us in the process.

Intent on controlling the circumstances around us, we are humbled repeatedly by the vicissitudes of life. This humbling can occupy either end of the spectrum of human experience. With a heavy heart, we may find ourselves surrendering to a force greater than ourselves. Or we may be on our knees, silently expressing gratitude for awe-inspiring gifts that gloriously reveal the profound beauty of life.

"Living Life" is divided into two parts. "Heartbreaking Moments" includes stories of love, courage, and compassion in the wake of unbearable loss. The transcendent stories in "Sacred Moments," full of hope and triumph, speak to the strength of the human spirit and the joy of the human experience.

14

JAMES AUTRY AND SALLY PEDERSON

Autry had a distinguished career at Meredith Corporation, where he was senior vice president and president of its Magazine Group. He's been active in many civic and charitable organizations, including a stint as chairman of the board of the Epilepsy Foundation of America, and he has worked with disability-rights groups for twenty-five years. Autry is the author of ten books, including The Book of Hard Choices; The Spirit of Retirement; *and* Life and Work: A Manager's Search for Meaning. *A founder of the Des Moines National Poetry Festival, Autry has published two books of poetry and was featured in Bill Moyers's special PBS series* The Power of the Word. *For more information, visit members.aol.com/jamesautry.*

Pederson is a former executive at Meredith Corporation, where she was the senior food editor of Better Homes and Gardens *magazine. She was elected lieutenant governor of Iowa in 1998 and re-elected to a second four-year term in 2002. A steadfast advocate for people with disabilities, she spearheaded numerous initiatives for healthcare and human services while in office. Pederson currently serves as a trustee of Union Theological Seminary in New York City and is chair of the Advisory Committee for REACH (Realizing Education and Career Hopes) at the University of Iowa.*

Autry's quotes are in regular type. *Pederson's quotes are in italics.*

S ally and I were married in 1982. Three years later, when our son Ronald was two years old, we knew something was terribly wrong. His subsequent diagnosis of autism, and my response to that diagnosis, changed everything in my life. Not only did it accelerate my process of awareness and consciousness, it profoundly changed my priorities. I was a highly paid senior corporate executive at Meredith Corp. and even had thoughts about becoming CEO some day. Instead, as I watched Ronald's struggle to find his place in the world, I realized that I couldn't do this anymore. I couldn't keep traveling twenty-two weeks a year. Sally and I sat down and agreed that as soon as we had enough saved to get by financially, I would take early retirement.

After Ron was born, I had planned to go back to work at Meredith as a food editor, but spending my career creating more recipes no longer held meaning for me. I had something more important to do. I wanted to make a difference for people living with disabilities.

We came to terms with the immediate reality of Ron's autism by simply doing what we had to do—the education, the speech therapy. I tried to communicate with Ron in ways that were not traditional, such as putting my head against his head at night while he slept and trying to visualize positive outcomes. As you do these things, it sinks in. You come to grips with it little by little. It's not an *Aha!* experience. You don't say, "Gee, I'm over the grief now." What you say is, "There's so much joy in this life that it overwhelms the grief."

Jim and I realized that we had to grieve for the child who was never going to be, but there is also this incredible joy at the child you do have. Ron has been a gift in many ways. He's also allowed me to do something more meaningful with my life than I could ever have imagined.

My sensitivity to the world, my approach to work, my creative writing, my relationship with my wife—almost everything shifted. Having a child with a disability creates great turmoil and conflict for some people, but it brought us even closer together. We knew that we didn't have any personal issues that were nearly as compelling as the need to work hard so that Ronald could find his place in the world and have as fulfilling and productive a life as possible.

On a very personal level, Ron's autism made me really appreciate my husband. He had been a very successful and prominent figure, but he was willing to set aside his needs and be extremely supportive to me, and that changed our relationship. It was very healthy for both of us. It made our love grow deeper and increased our appreciation for one another.

At the age of fifty-eight, when Ron was eight, I left Meredith Corp. so that I could spend more time supporting Sally and caring for our son. I credit Ronald with enabling me to let go of the corporate ambition and move toward a more centered and spiritual place. I realized that I hadn't been such a terrific father to my two older sons from my first marriage. I had worked all the time and was career obsessed—it's an old story and a cliché. Ronald's autism gave me an opportunity to be a better father. When Sally was elected to the office of Lieutenant Governor, I realized that that was a great gift to me—the gift to do all the childcare, pack the lunches, go on band trips, cook, shop, and pay the bills. It became a spiritual pursuit for me—finding the spiritual in everyday things.

We traded places. I used to be the one waiting for Jim to come home from the important work he was doing out there—and sometimes I resented it. Suddenly, he was at home waiting for me. It can be very demanding and frustrating to parent a child with special needs. Sometimes I wouldn't be home for dinner and couldn't even call Jim to let him know. If you're the person on the other end of that, it can make you feel like the other person isn't caring about you. The very fact that my husband took on that support role, and did it in such a loving and caring way, and never showed any signs that he was resentful, was a growth experience for me. We came to the conclusion that every marriage could benefit from this kind of role reversal because the experience helps you appreciate what your partner has been living.

I was already sensitive to disability issues and had published one book of poetry before Ronald was born. Eventually, Ronald's situation began to find expression in my life through my poetry (see "Learning to Pray" at the end of this story). I've also written quite a few essays about my experiences as a father of a child with a disability. It's a little irritating when people say, "Oh, you have a special child." That's their euphemism for saying "a child with a disability." Even though they're trying to be nice, "special" is a patronizing and pitying term. You realize that disability does not define you.

In my new book, I have an essay called "Time to Give Those Miracle Stories a Rest." I begin it by saying, "As a Christian and a father of a child with a disability, I want to say that Jesus didn't do us any big favors by healing all those people. Because in effect, he was saying, 'Well, you're not perfect the way you are, you need to be fixed.' I prefer Mr. Rogers, who said, 'I love you just the way you are.'" The point is, we have a huge cultural bias that people with disabilities are somehow lesser people and not as human as those who have all of their faculties.

In the 1998 Iowa gubernatorial race, after Tom Vilsack won a very close primary on Tuesday, he called the next day and set up an appointment to talk with Jim and me. Since I had been active in his primary campaign, he wanted to get our thoughts on what he should be looking for in a lieutenant governor. We were both on the phone and offered some suggestions about specific people he should consider and also what characteristics the ideal running mate would possess. At one point, he said, "Are you sitting down?

I'd like to ask you if you would consider being on my short list of running mates." This came out of nowhere. I laughed and said that I wasn't a political animal. I thought it was a very strange notion, but Jim passed me a note that said, "Sally, you should think about this." So we talked with Tom some more. I remember thinking that his short list probably had a hundred names on it and that this was simply flattery because he was never going to pick me. The next day, Tom asked if I could send him a résumé and answer some questions. He needed to pick his running mate by Saturday, which was when the Democratic convention would take place. By now I'm starting to think, Well, if I could be his running mate, then I could give voice to the things that I care very passionately about—education, special education, and services for people with disabilities. So I tried to convince myself that there were good reasons why I should want to be lieutenant governor.

Ronald's motor skills were, and still are, very deficient. He couldn't walk without falling and smacking his head on the sidewalk. I wanted to protect him, to catch him and keep him from falling. My wife was the courageous one. She said, "No, we've got to let him fall." We were constantly coaching and teaching him and conditioning his muscles. We spent hours with him sitting on a medicine ball, rolling him forward toward the floor, pulling his arms up and encouraging him, until finally, one day he put his arms up and caught himself.

Friday night at nine o'clock, Jim and I were having after-dinner coffee with friends at a restaurant. A waiter came over and said there was a phone call for me. This is all, of course, secret hush-hush. It was Tom, asking me to come down to his campaign headquarters so he could interview me. I excused myself, went down to his office, and was there until midnight. We had a great conversation and talked about our many shared interests, concerns, and values. At the end of the evening, he asked, "Will you be my running mate?"

I said, "If you think I'm the best person, then yes, I'll do it."

When I got home, Jim was asleep. I crawled into bed and said, "Well, you're sleeping with the next lieutenant governor of Iowa." After I told Jim what had happened, I proceeded to lie awake all night long thinking, Oh my God, what have I done? *I was really apprehensive about what I was getting myself into and whether I was up for the job. It was a great leap of faith.*

The sense of loss and grief over having a disabled child still goes on. Just a few months ago, Sally and I had a good cry together. It just hit us that there was still a long, hard road ahead for Ronald. He's now twenty-three years old, has his own apartment, and rides a bus every day to the Drake University Law School's legal clinic, where he scans court documents into a computer and manipulates them into a database for research by law students. He's doing as well as you could ever expect him to do, but he is still very juvenile in his behavior. There's residual grief that's always hanging there, but it isn't depressing. We have a lot of fun with Ronald; we really appreciate his talents and gifts. Still, it can be very wearing. It comes and goes, but it doesn't come very often.

During our eight years in office, I focused on initiatives and subject areas that most career politicians wouldn't be interested in because they weren't the kinds of issues that would move you ahead. But I didn't have any further political ambitions, so I had the luxury of doing what I wanted to do with the job. Fortunately, when you're in an office like that, you confer importance on whatever issue you give attention to. We redesigned the way we deliver services to people with disabilities. We passed a mental health parity bill requiring that all insurance companies provide the same kind of care for mental illness as they do for physical illness. At the end of our second term, as we were leaving office, I invited people from all over the state who work in the disability area to come to the capital to be honored and thanked. A minor thing, but I can't tell you how many people came through the line to receive their certificate and said, "No one has ever said 'thank you' to me before." So often, the people who are honored in our culture are people who already have status or fame or money. People who do extremely noble work for low wages and not much public acclamation also need to be honored, and I was given the opportunity to do that.

What you realize is that a person's disability doesn't say who he or she is as a human being. It is only a condition. I remember having a discussion with a vice president of human resources who had hearing loss in his left ear. I was advocating hiring people with disabilities, and he was arguing that we would lose productivity. So I deliberately started talking into his left ear. He kept turning, and I'd move. Finally, he said, "What are you doing?" I said, "You're a pretty productive person, right? Well, I'm just trying to show you that you're not so productive when I'm talking into your left ear. Your disability has to be accommodated. If somebody has a wheelchair, why can't we just lift the desk three inches so they can do the work?"

Having a child with a disability changes you. It changes the way you see the world, and it changes your priorities. As Ronald's life progressed, I saw where the gaps were. Not only was there a gap for my son, but there were also gaps for other children. I understood that it wasn't enough to make sure my son got what he needed; I had a responsibility to make the system better so that every child would have the opportunity to get the most out of education and the most out of life. Ronald has had an impact on so many lives. His joyful, exuberant, trusting personality has had a big impact on people and opened many hearts. But he's also had an impact on people he's never met because of the way he opened my heart and made me see that I can give meaning to his disability by helping others.

Learning to Pray

Ronald has heard people pray,
the ministers at church,
his grandfather at family gatherings,
me at the dinner table,
and he knows there's supposed to be something important
about those words and phrases,
but he doesn't get them right,
the prayers;
of course he doesn't get a lot of things right.
"Grateful God," he says,
"Thank you for my ceiling fan
and my lawn mower and my cat . . ."

Once, for no reason I could discern,
he stopped cutting the grass,
let the mower engine die,
raised hands to face and said,
"You are a grateful God for giving me this Lawn Boy."
And in the Lord's Prayer he says,
"Hallowed be my name."

I used to think I should teach him to pray
the way everyone else does
but lately I don't know,
lately I find myself asking,
"How do I know that God is not
also to be grateful?"
Lately, I think less about God's majesty
and more about Ronald's struggle
to make sense of his place in this world,
never mind the next world.

Lately, I hear myself praying,
"Grateful God safely tucked away in Heaven,
we are thankful that Ronald
(hallowed be his name)
has come to live among us
in order that we may learn
how to face our disabilities,
how to find joy in ceiling fans and lawn mowers,
and how to pray.
Amen."

—Jim Autry

15

ECHO BODINE

Bodine, a psychic, spiritual healer, ghostbuster, and author, offers psychic development and healing classes at her Minneapolis teaching and healing center. Her abilities include clairvoyance (the gift of seeing), clairaudience (the gift of hearing), and clairsentience (the gift of sensing). Her eight books include A Still Small Voice: A Psychic's Guide to Awakening Intuition; The Key: Unlock Your Psychic Abilities; *and* Echoes of the Soul: The Soul's Journey Beyond the Light. *For more information, visit www.echobodine.com.*

When I was a sophomore in college, I found out I was pregnant. When my boyfriend and I talked about getting married, my inner voice very adamantly said, *No!* But I pretended I didn't hear it and kept on trying to make this really difficult situation more workable for me, my boyfriend, and our families. Our premarital counselor said that, even though we were both young, we could probably make it work. But all along, my intuition kept saying, *No, no, no, this is not the way to go.* And, deep down, I knew I had to listen to it.

So even though I wanted to get married and keep my baby, I said no to my boyfriend. It was very hard to explain to everyone that I was saying no because that's what felt right to me. It made sense to my mom, who taught me how to live by my intuition, but it didn't make sense to my boyfriend or anybody else.

In 1968, it was pretty shameful to be nineteen and an unwed mother, so I went off to California and told everybody I had transferred to a different college. Throughout the pregnancy, whenever I would rebel and think, *I'm going to keep this baby*, my intuition kept saying, *No, you're not*. And I would get the word *adoption* every time. Even though I had made arrangements with an adoption agency, in the back of my mind I kept thinking that when it came right down to it, I was going to take my baby home with me. Sometimes, out of desperation, I thought, *Maybe the day my son is born, my intuition will tell me, okay, now you can keep him.*

My son was born on a gloomy day in San Francisco. I've never lived a harder day in my life. I laid in my hospital bed crying and pleading with my intuition, *Can I please, please bring my baby home?* But it very clearly said, *No. Adoption.* My boyfriend was still suggesting that we get married and raise our baby, and I had a strong desire and a strong will to do that too. My parents had told me they would support me if I kept my baby, and the family friends I was living with in San Francisco even came to my hospital room and asked me to let them raise my son.

Yet, in spite of everything the world was saying, my inner voice told me to trust its guidance and that it would all work out some day. I knew I had to trust my intuition, but it was the most difficult thing I ever had to do. I cried, "Please, God, you have to talk to me; you have to tell me how this is going to turn out if I place him for adoption." But all I heard was, *It's going to be okay.*

I knew I couldn't hold him. I knew that if I did, my will would take over. The last time they wheeled me to the nursery window to see him, the candy striper innocently said, "Oh, did you get your baby's pictures?" I remember thinking, *Oh my God, will somebody please get me out of here? I can't stand this kind of pain!*

In the years that followed, there were many, many moments when I wondered if I should have kept my baby instead of listening to my intuition, especially since I never had any more children after that. And yet, my inner voice would always say, *It will be okay. Someday, it will be okay.*

Today, I'm thankful that I can say it did indeed turn out okay and that both his father and I no longer have any doubt that I did the right thing. In my most recent book, *A Still Small Voice,* I write about finding my son twenty-five years later. He was raised in a wonderful family, and we now have a wonderful relationship. I also still get along very well with his biological father. In fact, in September, the two of us went to our son's wedding.

Our intuition doesn't tell us why it's telling us what to do. It just gives us a direction, which is why it's so hard to follow. We humans want the path laid out for us. We want to see it clearly, and then we'll make our decision. But that's not how it works. It's really about surrendering to God and doing what we came here to do, even though we don't know at the time where our path is leading us.

I really struggled with whether or not to share such a personal story, but then I realized that if someone reading this is faced with a difficult situation, and their inner voice is guiding them to do something that makes no sense to them, maybe my story will speak to them and tell them, *Follow it anyway.*

16

FRANK DEFORD

Deford has authored fifteen books, including The Entitled, *a novel about an old baseball manager, a young superstar, and the glamorous realm of modern sport, and* An American Summer, *a novel that explores the friendship between a young boy and a young woman with polio in the summer of '54. Deford is widely regarded as the consummate sportswriter of his era, most notably for his award-winning work in* Sports Illustrated. *He also appears regularly on National Public Radio's* Morning Edition *and on HBO's* RealSports. *His daughter's struggle with cystic fibrosis, which is poignantly documented in his book,* Alex: The Life of a Child, *led him to serve as national chairman of the Cystic Fibrosis Foundation for fifteen years. He is now chairman emeritus of that organization. Frank can be reached at frank6de@aol.com.*

An excerpt from *Alex: The Life of a Child*:

Now that I was there, they were ready to make the chest incision and insert the tube. The first time Alex had a collapsed lung—a pneumothorax, it was called—she had been given a large dosage of painkiller, and it really knocked her out; she slept for hours and was groggy many more. Thereafter, even though she was so frightened of pain, she seemed all the more frightened that she might never wake up, and so she told the doctors only to give her a local.

We did not know it at the time, but this would be the last occasion when Alex would—could—have the tubes inserted. [My wife]

Carol and I, and Alex, feared that it would keep happening, again and again, the final cruel indignity, but what we did not know was that, after this time, [Dr.] Tom Dolan doubted that her body could stand the trauma of another cut. There was so little left of her.

And so I carried Alex into her treatment room. By then she had prepared herself fairly well, but as soon as she saw that stark table where she was to lie and receive her shot and her incision, she stiffened and was the little girl again. "No, not yet! Not yet!" she cried, and she clung to me as tight as she ever had.

I remember noticing that both nurses there turned away from us at that moment, because, for all they might see, day after day in a hospital, there was such an awful intimacy to Alex's gesture that they could not bear to intrude on us. I only held Alex and tried to comfort her more.

And, in time, when she had composed herself, she said, "All right. I'm ready now." And so she was.

So I started to lay her down where they would cut her open. And in that moment, I could not hold back any longer; one tear fell from all those welling in my eyes. And Alex saw it, saw my face as I bent to put her down. Softer, but urgently, she cried out, "Wait!" We all thought she was only delaying the operation again, but instead, so gently, so dearly, she reached up, and with an angel's touch, swept the tear from my face.

I will never know such sweetness again in all my life.

"Oh, my little Daddy, I'm so sorry," is what she said.

One nurse turned and bowed her head and began to sob. The other could not even stay in the room. She ran off to compose herself. It was some time before we could get going again.

That was one of the most powerful of all the moments I shared with Alex. She was in pain, and she knew there was going to be even more pain. And yet, she was more concerned about me.

"Oh, my little Daddy, don't worry about me." That was super-human. We tend to use that word—*superhuman*—when somebody has done something marvelous, but it can also relate to something spiritual, beyond normal human capacity. And, in my mind, in that moment, Alex was about as far as you could get above human. And it was not naiveté. It was not childhood ignorance. She was old enough to know what was going on. It was just selflessness.

Obviously, I think that Alex was particularly something special, but I have met enough other children with cystic fibrosis and other diseases to know that a great many of them take on a certain maturity, that they are somehow imbued with a spirit that can infuse us. It's probably because they're around adults more and because they have to deal with a grown-up situation. Yet they can drift back rather quickly and become childlike again if you put them in a childhood situation. It's almost a bifurcated kind of life. Put Alex in a peaceful setting with a friend and dolls, and she was as childish as anybody could be.

But put her under pressure and those qualities, that wisdom, that maturity, came into play. Those who are most frail, most vulnerable, can sometimes exude the greatest strength. It may be a God-given thing they need in order to get by. It's also a kind of armor they put on to help the people around them because there's nothing worse than seeing your child in pain and dying. Here she was so young, so wasted away at the end, yet there was a power to her, a living spirituality that I experienced when I was with her that was stronger than anything I felt after she was gone.

It's important to note that an extraordinarily high number of marriages break up when a child becomes sick and dies. It's because both the mother and the father need the same thing, and they can't get it from each other. It's really hard and you can't imagine what it's like until you've been put through that fire.

I think that, instinctively, Alex tried to help us get through those difficult times.

Alex died in January, and that summer my wife suggested to me that we adopt. I should add that, every night, when Alex would say her prayers, she would always end up asking God to help the poor children in other countries and to help bring them to the United States. Where this came from, I don't know.

Another excerpt:

I knew in my heart that I was cool to the idea, and as long as I was, it was wrong to pursue it. I tried to figure out why I was so reluctant to consider adoption, and finally one day, when I was out at the grave discussing this with Alex, I understood: I didn't think it would be fair to Alex. She was my daughter, my child. She had been the one born to grow up in our house, in our family. Bad enough that she should be sick and die; now we should haul some-one else in, some stranger, to take her place? To me, that would be the ultimate inequity, the final injustice. I just couldn't bring another child in to replace Alex, and, finally, I told Carol that, directly. That was the end of it. I was sorry, but I couldn't do that.

Carol didn't say anything. I went on. Somehow, worst of all, I said, was the way Alex loved little babies, and she would love a lit-tle baby girl the most of all. So here she would not only be replaced by a little girl—that was bad enough—but she would also be the one of us who couldn't enjoy the little girl. That made it crueler still.

Carol just listened to me. It was a lovely summer evening, and we were sitting out on the patio, having a drink. [Our son] Chris was off somewhere in the neighborhood, playing ball. This is the way it always had been. He would go off, but Alex would get all dressed up in her summer finery, snap on a hundredweight of assorted costume jewelry, and come out and have a Coke with us.

Sometimes she would put on her Chinese lounging pajamas and act particularly grown-up. It would be fairly soon after her evening therapy, and she probably wouldn't have to cough unless something made her laugh really hard.

"I'm sorry," I said to Carol. "Do you understand? I just can't do that to Alex."

"You know," Carol said, "if we did get a baby—if—"

"Carol, you heard what I said."

"Just listen to me. If we did get a baby, you know we could never get one in the States, and it would have to come from some country way out of the way."

"I know that," I said. "A lot of them come from South America now."

"Some very poor country," Carol said, and I nodded. Then suddenly, she reached over and took my hand in hers. "Do you remember Alex's prayer, what she said every night?"

"Sure I do."

"You remember the part she made up herself, the part she'd always say: 'And God, please take care of our country, and bring some of the poor people to our country, and make the other countries rich like us.'" There were tears in my eyes even before Carol had finished. A baby would be an answer to Alex's prayer as much as it would be our new child.

Indeed, we did adopt a little girl from the Philippines. Scarlet is now twenty-five and working as a graphic artist in New York for a large magazine company. It's almost mystical and magical all the things that allowed us to adopt her. There were so many hurdles, none of which we should have gotten by. It was almost as if Alex was pulling the strings from heaven. I hate to be corny, but you almost had to think that because so many things had to fall into place.

The most dramatic thing that happened was that the first family that the child was offered to turned her down because she was a girl and they wanted a boy. That would've ended it right there. And there were all these other obstacles that should've prevented it so that you had to think there was divine guidance and that Alex had some role in it, not only to help this little girl, but to help our family stay together. You could say it was a spiritual experience, but I'd like to think it was even something beyond that.

One more thing. Alex always called me "my little Daddy." It was very appropriate because the tables were often reversed. It almost had that upside-down flavor of her being the parent and me being the child. It's curious but I, too, have a genetic lung condition. It's not cystic fibrosis, but I may have to eventually deal with some of the same challenges that she dealt with so magnificently. I just know that whenever my time comes, I will be so ashamed of myself unless I can be as courageous as she was.

17

JIM MacLAREN

MacLaren, a motivational speaker and author, has triumphed over two horrific accidents that would have destroyed a lesser man. At twenty-two, he was a Yale All-American athlete and aspiring actor when his motorcycle was broadsided by a New York City bus. Dead on arrival, he woke up after an eight-day coma to find his left leg amputated below the knee. Inspired by a book about triathlons, he became the fastest one-legged endurance athlete on the planet, routinely finishing ahead of most able-bodied athletes. Eight years later, a van plowed into him during a race, rendering him a quadriplegic. Since then, MacLaren has created the Choose Life Foundation, earned two master's degrees, and is working toward his Ph.D. in mythology and depth psychology. For more information, visit www.jimmaclaren.com.

I was having an early morning cup of coffee on Saturday, June 5, 1993, the day before a major triathlon in Mission Viejo, California. I was sitting on my girlfriend's porch in Boulder, Colorado, reflecting on a pretty heady book I was reading, *The Secret Doctrine* by H. P. Blavatsky. Although I was up on a porch, covered by trees, I could hear families walking to breakfast with their children on the street below. It was such a beautiful, pristine summer day. I was gazing at the trees and the huge rock faces in the distance and looking back over the eight years since I had lost my leg. I remember thinking, *Wow, I've really reinvented myself. I'm a professional triathlete. ESPN is following me in the race tomorrow, and I'm traveling around the world, racing and giving motivational talks*. And it hit me. I thought, *Wow, I'm back in it. I'm back in life*.

Out of nowhere, I started crying. My girlfriend, and training partner, came out on the porch with a cup of coffee, saw me crying, and asked, "What's the matter?"

I smiled through tears and said, "Nothing is the matter. I'm crying because I'm happy. Something amazing is about to happen to me. I can just feel it."

Fast-forward eighteen hours later. I wake up early, get to the race, and again, I'm feeling wonderful because I'm being announced along with the top pros. The race starts. I finish the mile swim and hop on my bike. A couple miles into the bike ride on a closed course, I'm stretched out on my aerodynamic handlebars, just flying. I assumed the people watching were applauding until I realized they were screaming. I look over to my left, and coming right at me is the grill of a black van. I learned later that a traffic marshal had misjudged my speed approaching the intersection and had directed the van to cross the street.

Life in these moments really slows down. I remember thinking, *Okay, if I pedal one click faster, I can beat this guy across the intersection*. The last things I remember hearing were people screaming and the driver hitting his accelerator instead of his brakes. He struck my back wheel. I was thrown from my bike, flew headfirst into a signpost, and broke my neck.

None of that I remember. I woke up in the ambulance, still in race mode, feeling the adrenaline. I was in the same state of mind I had been in eight years earlier. When I first woke up after getting hit by that bus and saw that my left leg was missing, I thought, *Oh, okay, cool, your left leg's gone*. And I went back to sleep. When I woke up the day after that, that's when my ego and brain started freaking out.

So when I came to in the ambulance, I knew right away that my leg didn't work. But I remember thinking, *Oh, maybe I'm just a paraplegic. Maybe I'll be able to wheelchair race. And I could go beat Jim Knaub* (who held all the wheelchair marathon records). Then I blacked out again.

The next thing I know, I'm in the hospital, outside the OR. A doctor is holding my hand. He tells me straight, "Look, you're a C5-C6 quad, which means that you broke your neck right up around your ears, and you're never going to move or feel again from the chest down for the rest of your life." At that moment, there was some aspect of me that felt that if he never let go of my hand, I'd be okay. But, of course, he had to let go because they wheeled me into the OR. That was the start of multiple surgeries and months of being in the ICU. Basically, the inferno had begun. It was hell. When a buddy from Yale came to see me, I rolled over, looked at him, and said, "I don't know if I can do this again." Because I didn't.

As I look back—it's been fourteen years now—there aren't a lot of days where I feel great physically. There are a lot of things that I've lost—my fiancée, much of my independence, the use of my left shoulder due to a failed rotator cuff surgery. But that's life. I had a choice: I could lose myself to my body or learn to live beyond it. I found my strength by saying and believing that I am not my body. I am a man. I am alive, as alive as anybody who's dunking a basketball or scoring a touchdown or hugging their child.

Even though both accidents were devastating at the time, I now view them as gifts and not tragedies. Granted, it might have been easier to say that eighteen months ago because the last year and a half has been literally miserable. During trips to the hospital, I picked up mono, chronic fatigue syndrome, and an antibiotic-resistant bacteria, which is a real trip. So I've been spending most every day getting up, going to the bathroom, and going back to bed. But even through those tough times, magic happens.

Even though I'm now considered an "incomplete quad" because I have full sensation and movement to varying degrees, I'm still in chronic pain 24/7. Mornings are the worst—I wake up and feel like wet cement plugged into the wall. If I were going to think, *Okay, the rest of my day is going to go exactly how I feel right now, I'd never get up.* But that's not what I do. I start moving my leg a little bit, and my bed becomes an exercise mat. And when I'm up in my chair and sitting on the porch, it's a hundred times better than the way I felt when I woke up.

I've learned to engage life on whatever level I can, whether it's doing sit-ups in bed or calling friends during the three or four hours it takes for me to get ready in the morning. I've made a ritual out of it. Engaging life, feeling that life force surge through me, helps me recapture the sort of feeling I had in Boulder the day before that big race, that something amazing was going to happen to me. Well, something amazing did happen. Maybe not the way Merriam-Webster defines it, but yeah, something pretty amazing happened to me.

Granted, some days are harder than others. I was on an NPR radio show with my friend Bob Kerrey, the former U.S. senator from Nebraska who's missing a leg. The radio host asked Bob if he considers the loss of his leg a gift, and Bob said, "Yeah, I believe it's a gift, but some mornings it's a gift I'd like to wake up without." I feel the same way. There are times I don't like the way my life went, but that doesn't mean that I'm not in love with life.

So, yeah, even though the last eighteen months have been hell, I can still say, as objectively as possible, that I wouldn't trade what happened to me. Having to admit to my own dependency and vulnerability actually made me more powerful. Why? It dawned on me that acknowledging your wounds and vulnerabilities and becoming more conscious and knowledgeable about yourself actually make you a stronger person. I've learned how to let people in who really love me and say, "I'm hurting, and I'm human, and I need some help." If I can look at my life truthfully and accept everything that's happened to me, then I can believe that I'm always going to be okay. What I believe in obviously works, and it's in my soul, because otherwise, I would've tried to step over my balcony.

People often tell me things like, "You have such a strong will," or "You have such an amazing attitude," but there's just never been a thought in me about, *Boy, if I was just the way I used to be, I wouldn't be going through all this BS*. It's always been, *Okay, here's a new challenge; let me figure it out, let me face it*. For me, the journey has always been about going deeper and becoming more of a human being. And you know what? Just once in a while being okay with the fact that it's fricking hard. It's just hard, and it's not fair. And when I say that, I'm saying that for everybody in the world. Somehow, we were brought up to believe that life is fair, and that if we're good, then it's all going to always be good. But stuff happens. Is it fair what's happened to me? No, of course not. So what? I still have to get up in the morning. It's not about overcoming adversity; it's about living with adversity.

There's a myth from Finland that embracing depth psychology, or probing your own depths, is like setting out across a thousand-mile tundra by yourself. It's not easy. It doesn't always mean that you get the girl or that you get to walk, but maybe it gives you peace.

18

DONALD SCHNELL

Schnell, a financial lender and investor, authored The Initiation, *a memoir of his encounter in India with Babaji, the legendary deathless guru. Initiated as a swami in India in 1997, Schnell also coauthored* Fitonics for Life *with his wife, Marilyn Diamond (coauthor of* Fit for Life*), which offers a comprehensive program for total wellness. Donald can be reached at premababa1@aol.com.*

I met Margaret in a Black History night class at Fayetteville State University. She needed the credit for the nursing degree she was working toward. We were both stationed at Fort Bragg, North Carolina, proud members of the 82nd Airborne. She was twenty-four, five years older than me, and a divorced African-American mother of two—four-year-old Joe and five-year-old "Little Maggie."

Nobody messed with Margaret. She was a loner who had clearly had a hard life. She wasn't well educated, but she was very bright and a good conversationalist. You could see a fire to succeed in her eyes. In attitude and appearance, she reminded me of Whoopi Goldberg, albeit a bit stockier with a short military haircut.

Did I mention her willpower? After watching me add significant muscle to my frame with a rigorous weight-training regimen, she lost forty pounds in ninety days on a strict tuna-and-water diet. Wow! The discipline it took to be in the military, go to school, raise two kids on your own, and eat nothing but tuna for three months was astonishing.

On top of all that, this was 1974, and while women could technically join the military, the men in charge at Fort Bragg, or "Little Hell" as we grunts called it, made it clear that women were less than welcome. As the only white soldier in an all-black unit, courtesy of the military's ongoing plan to integrate the army, I could sympathize with Margaret's struggle to fit in. If it hadn't been for my roommate, James Bailey, sticking up for me, my time in the barracks would have been unpleasant, to say the least.

So I was glad when James invited Margaret to join the early-morning zazen—or "sitting Zen"—group I had started. Zazen is the practice that Buddha used to attain spiritual enlightenment. The requirements are demanding. The meditator sits kneeling, Japanese-style on the heels, the chin parallel to the floor, and every effort is made to hold a perfectly erect position. You sit absolutely still and keep the attention focused on the present moment, the breath, and nothing else. It's a powerful technique used by many martial artists because it sharpens the mind and body very quickly.

Our days were full, so we would have to be up by 4 AM in order to get an hour of zazen in. Soon, we had five meditating military monks in our zendo, the space where the group practice of Zen takes place. As more soldiers kept joining, we moved from the barracks to a recreation hall, where we practiced around the pool tables. Most of us wore just a T-shirt and combat fatigue pants. It could be quite cold that early in the morning, but in zazen, you learn to ignore the needs of the body. What's a little cold compared to the goal of liberation and spiritual enlightenment?

I used a pool cue as a kyokyaku stick, also known as the stick of compassion, to keep the fires of meditation burning. The roshi, or Zen priest, uses the stick if your posture weakens or you start to fall asleep. He strikes you on either the right or left shoulder. After you are struck, you bow to the roshi in gratitude for keeping you on the path to enlightenment. The loud "crack" of the kyokyaku stick has been known to bring many a monk into spiritual enlightenment. Because the crack happens in the moment, it forces you to awaken into the moment. Remember, Buddha means "the awakened one." To remind others of the transitory nature of life is an act of great compassion.

The fact that Margaret would get up so early and put the time in to sit Zen with us was exceptional considering all her other commitments. She never missed a morning's sesshin, as they were called, so we all knew something was amiss when she didn't show up one day. That afternoon, we found out she had been diagnosed with an advanced case of leukemia. She was in great pain, and the doctors gave her only a short time to live.

Remarkably, Margaret continued to attend sesshin for as long as she could. She said that the meditation helped her manage the pain and get through her day. For all of us in sesshin, Margaret became the Buddha by virtue of her indomitable will. Her inner strength was incredible. Every day, no matter how she was feeling, she asked for an extra dose of the compassion stick from me.

Inevitably, the morning came when Margaret failed to show. I found her in the hospital later that day, practicing her zazen in spite of the heavy pain medication. She asked me if there was a way I could bring the sesshin to her hospital room. "Of course," I told her. Thereafter, nine of us gathered at the hospital early every morning to keep the sesshin going. The rest of the group continued without us at the recreation hall. Everyone wanted to participate with Margaret, but we couldn't bring that many people into her room.

Then we ran into Nurse Leona, a Christian fundamentalist with a temper that matched the color of her red hair. Leona let us know in no uncertain terms that she didn't want any disturbances on her floor. We explained that what we were doing was spiritual, that it was Margaret's religion, and that we would be extremely quiet. But she wanted no part of what she perceived to be Satan's work and went to great lengths to have us expelled.

Leona complained to the hospital chaplain that a non-Christian element was invading the peace of the hospital. She enlisted the help of a sympathetic second lieutenant who put me on all-night guard duty with no relief. He then sent James and me into the field for a week of survival training with no food.

Margaret persevered while awaiting our return. As a group, we held our ground with clear, quiet, Zen authority. We wanted to be strong for her. In order to see Margaret and help her with her Zen practice, I was required to fill out several forms declaring my religion to be Zen Buddhism, although I was, in truth, a Christian practicing Zen Buddhism. I had to do the same for Margaret and the rest of the group. I was also told that this admission would affect my ability to keep my top-secret clearance. It was clearly a threat, designed to discourage me, but Margaret's one-pointed determination that the group must continue as a whole inspired me to do whatever had to be done. She courageously modeled the truth that one's spiritual discipline must be maintained at all costs.

Fortunately, one of our members, a seasoned master sergeant and former Green Beret, stepped up and made things right. The master sergeant was one of the first people in my life who completely impressed me. He was all soldier—tall, erect, muscular, all spit and polish, an African-American king. No one crossed him, but not because he was mean. On the contrary, he was kind and fair, and he was known to be color-blind. He was so decorated for heroism and carried himself with such regal dignity that his word on the base was essentially law.

The master sergeant went straight to Fort Bragg's head chaplain. Notwithstanding the fact that the head chaplain had a higher rank than he did, the master sergeant, who was in charge of the motor pool, made it clear that if the chaplain wanted to continue to receive the cleanest and finest transportation every day, he would have to play ball. I suspect he also made it clear that he was aware of some of the married chaplain's shenanigans with one of the young female soldiers. At that time, sexual harassment had not yet become an open issue in the military, but the master sergeant had a case to make, and the chaplain knew it. Much to Margaret's relief, and to the chagrin of Nurse Leona, we were granted clearance to report to the hospital at 8 AM to honor our spiritual practice of zazen for two full hours.

I'm sure our practice inspired a number of double takes. Imagine a typical military doctor striding into the room with "Hello, how we doing today?" only to find nine soldiers sitting on the floor in perfect, silent zazen around the bed in which sat his patient, totally still and erect. When doing a sesshin, we would not even veer from our practice to acknowledge the doctor or anyone else who entered the space. The sesshin was our time to focus on our inner divinity. Often, Margaret's two young children, Joe and Little Maggie, would participate by sitting on the master sergeant's lap. The kids behaved because their mother had taught them the rules. After a few days, Margaret's doctor got into the spirit of things. He realized he was walking into a zendo temple. He came in quietly and performed his examination serenely. It was a total shift in typical hospital protocol.

As Margaret grew weaker, she took advantage of her tilting mattress to keep her upright. She would just lie back with the bed tilted at the proper angle. In Japan, when a person is dying, a screen that shows the Buddha traveling to heaven is placed in front of that person. The screen is used as a reminder of where we are to focus during our final journey. I told her about the screen and its symbolism—and desperately wished I could provide one for her—but we both knew it wasn't likely that we'd find a Buddha screen in the Bible Belt of North Carolina. I was touched when she told me that I was her screen, her reminder to look to heaven and follow the Buddha.

The doctors were amazed at how calm and accepting Margaret was about her impending death. Her poise and grace were extraordinary. She was taking about one-third of the pain medication that similar patients would take. On some days, she took none at all. They didn't understand how that was possible. Since Margaret had no family to speak of, the master sergeant was busy making arrangements with social organizations to take care of Joe and Little Maggie.

One spring morning, we arrived to find Margaret's bed empty. Nurse Leona told us somewhat cruelly that we were no longer allowed in the hospital. We learned from the doctor that Margaret had died peacefully around 4 AM. He said she rang the bell for assistance, but when they got there she had already died. They found her bed tilted up and Margaret sitting comfortably with a peaceful look on her face—a Zen Buddhist to the end.

Margaret's death hit us hard. Buddha said that the world was suffering, sorrow, and illusion, and that anything we cling to in the world, including our physical body, is going to pass. If we cling to it and attach to it, we're going to suffer. But we couldn't ignore Margaret's death by saying, "Hey, we're all Zen Buddhists, and it's all an illusion." Someone who we loved and cared about, who had two young children, had died. We were all novices and didn't know how to process that. By her powerful example, Margaret showed us how the transcendence of suffering lies within each of us. She showed us how to maintain one foot in compassion and one foot in total clarity.

Margaret had a military funeral, disguised as a weapons training procedure. Military funerals for ordinary soldiers are not customary, but all the arrangements had been quietly made by the master sergeant. The chaplain was absent, so the master sergeant read the Twenty-third Psalm. I was given the privilege of folding the American flag that adorned Margaret's simple casket and presenting it to her children. I walked toward them in the slow, dignified, carefully measured steps of the walking form of Zen meditation known as kinhin. A lump formed in my throat that I couldn't control.

"Your mother was so strong, Joey," I whispered as I knelt close to him. His big sad eyes looked directly into mine. "Keep this flag to always remind you of how strong you are and how strong your mother was."

"Is my Mommy coming back?" he asked.

With tears streaming down my face, I told him, "She's with God now."

As Joe took the flag in his hands, he stood straight at attention while tears rolled down his cheeks. Standing beside him, I rested my palm upon Little Maggie's head. She reached up for me to hold her, which I did. Her little arms squeezed around me in the tightest grip I'd ever known. She buried her head in my shoulder and sobbed.

Rifle shots rang out, unexpectedly, like the crack of the kyokyaku stick. For me, and I'm sure for most of the zendo group, they symbolized Buddha's teaching to awaken in this very moment to the preciousness of life.

19

STEPHEN SIMON

Simon has produced or supervised the production of nearly two dozen films, including Somewhere in Time, *starring Christopher Reeve, and* What Dreams May Come, *starring Robin Williams. Most recently, he produced and directed the film version of Neale Donald Walsch's bestseller,* Conversations with God, *as well as* Indigo, *an independent film about spiritually gifted children. Simon is a cofounder of the Spiritual Cinema Circle, which delivers meaningful, spiritually-themed movies to its members every month. He expresses his passion for the emerging category of spiritual cinema in his book,* The Force Is With You: Mystical Movie Messages That Inspire Our Lives. *For more information, visit www.cwgthemovie.com and www.spiritual cinemacircle.com.*

By October 1998, I had become incredibly disenchanted with the Hollywood film industry. It was beginning to dawn on me that I needed to do something different. It had taken me a long time to come to this point—I had been involved in over twenty films as either a producer or as an executive over the last twenty-five years.

We had just released *What Dreams May Come*, a film that had literally been a twenty-year odyssey in my life. That's how difficult it was to get spiritual films made in the Hollywood system. Yet films that were of the heart and of the spirit were the only kind I wanted to make.

From a production standpoint, *What Dreams May Come* was an incredibly painful experience. For example, I wound up having a six-week argument with PolyGram, who had financed the film, about the word *consciousness*. They didn't want the word *consciousness* in the film. They wanted to change it to *awareness*. I finally won that battle.

Right after the film was released, I got a phone call from PolyGram. They had been contacted by a theater owner in Milwaukee, Wisconsin, who had in turn been contacted by the father of a terminally ill teenager. She was too ill to get out of the house to see *What Dreams May Come* but desperately wanted to see it. The father wanted to know if it was possible for a videotape to be made and sent to him.

To their credit, the people at PolyGram were incredibly gracious about being willing to do it. We got a videotape made and couriered it to this gentleman's house. His name is Chuck Weber, and he was and still is a contractor in Milwaukee. I called his home number and left a message that we were sending him the tape and that we hoped it would do everything he wanted it to do.

I didn't hear anything back for a while, but a week or two later, I got a phone call from a friend of Chuck's who told me that Chuck had received the tape and that Amanda, his daughter, did see the film but had passed away only a couple days after.

One day, a week or two later, I picked up the phone, and a really nice guy on the other side of the phone said, "This is Chuck Weber. Is this Stephen Simon?" We wound up having a conversation that changed the course of my life forever. Chuck had been a single father. I had been a single father for many years myself, so we had an immediate connection there. I had four daughters, but Amanda had been Chuck's only child.

Chuck told me that Amanda was seventeen years old, had been diagnosed with a very rare combination of two different forms of cancer, and had been very, very brave about her illness right up until the end. But she had gotten very frightened as the time came for her transition because she didn't have a frame of reference as to where she was going to go. After seeing the ads for *What Dreams May Come* on television, she told her dad she really wanted to see the film, and that's why he had called.

Chuck said that when the courier showed up with the film, the courier told him that PolyGram had instructed him to stay in the house while they watched the film. But when the courier saw what the situation was, which was Amanda in a hospice bed in the living room, he was gracious enough to say, "Listen, here's the video. Call me when you're done with it, and I'll come back and get it tomorrow."

The courier left, and Chuck showed the film to Amanda and some of her friends. Chuck said to me, "Stephen, I have to be honest with you. I didn't watch the film, and I may never have the courage to watch the film. But I watched Amanda watch the film. And when it got to the painted-world sequence, I saw all the fear disappear from my daughter's eyes. She became completely peaceful. The next day, she asked me to take her out to a park. She wanted to see the fall colors one more time. And the day after that, she died very peacefully."

He then added, "Listen, this is what I need to tell you. I don't know if this is a good film or not. I don't know what the critics think of it. I don't know if it's doing any business or if it isn't. And I don't care. What I need to say to you is that it changed the last two days of my daughter's life. And that is the only success that you should ever strive for."

As Chuck was talking, everything crystallized for me. Right then and there, I committed myself to only making films that deal with the experience of what humanity can be when we operate at our very best. It was a deeply emotional and spiritual experience for me. And everything I have done since then has been dedicated to the memory of Amanda Weber.

The connection I felt with Chuck turned out to be a lasting one. He became a very dear family friend and is now known in our family as Uncle Chuck. My daughters have a lot of Amanda's clothing as well as her record collection and her crystals. And Chuck has become a very dear, very close friend of mine.

20

MIKE VEECK

Veeck, a third-generation baseball executive, is a minority owner in five minor-league teams and a consultant to five others. His grandfather, William Veeck Sr., was a sportswriter who became president of the Chicago Cubs. His father, Bill Veeck, was a legendary maverick who owned, at various times, the Cleveland Indians, St. Louis Browns, and Chicago White Sox. Mike Veeck held major-league marketing positions for the Chicago White Sox, Tampa Bay Devil Rays, Florida Marlins, and Detroit Tigers. Founder of the Veeck Promotional Seminar, he released a corporate training video based on his "Fun is Good" philosophy as well as a Fun Is Good *book. For more information, visit www.funisgood.net.*

In October 1998, I accepted a job as senior vice president of marketing for the Tampa Bay Devil Rays and moved my family to Florida. When my daughter, Rebecca, who was almost seven, had a wellness check before starting school, she couldn't read the big "E" on the eye chart. Of course, being a Veeck, we thought she was hamming it up, but she started crying and said, "I really can't read the eye chart." My wife Libby and I took her to a specialist right away, and it was confirmed that Rebecca had retinitis pigmentosa, a genetic degenerative eye disease. It was incurable. She was going to go blind. It was just a question of how fast.

In the course of a few moments, your world changes forever. Suddenly, there's something wrong with your perfect child. And it shakes you. She received a lifetime sentence, and you're thinking,

We'll win on appeal. I could hardly pronounce retinitis pigmentosa, but I had this feeling that by sheer will, by hoping and by praying and by helping in the small ways that each of us are able to do, Rebecca could overcome her disease. Well, that's poppycock. It quickly became apparent that this was a seven-day-a-week, twenty-four-hours-a-day thing. And that's what wears you out—the battering—because it's just continual.

Little things we had wondered about now made perfect sense. She had always held books right up to her eyes; we thought it was a little quirk. And she had this cute little thing: when you'd come up, she'd turn her head and look at you out of the corner of her eye; I just thought she was trying to be Veronica Lake. But here she'd been, living in shadows her whole life.

The instinct that's almost Neanderthal, that's ingrained in all of us, is that you take care of your family, and you especially take care of your daughter. But in this case, you're unable to do it. You're suspended in a kind of animated disbelief. You hear the doctor's words, but they don't really sink into your soul.

Of course, I made all the classic overreactions; I bought her a television monitor that magnified print. I bought her a virtual-reality headpiece. Things like that. None of which she used because Libby and I had long before planted the seeds of raising a very independent child whose attitude was *I refuse to take any prisoners. I'm not giving in to this.*

Even so, for the first ninety days after Rebecca's diagnosis, it was very difficult for her. Suddenly, there were monsters under her bed. She was crying in the middle of the night and wanting to crawl into bed with us. I would open my bedroom door and find her sleeping outside our door or under a picture of my dad, her "guardian angel." And always, the lights were on, because even though she kept up this tremendously brave front for us, she was afraid that if she went to sleep in the dark, she might wake up blind. And if the lights were off, she wouldn't know if she had gone completely blind or if it was just dark. I was so stupid; I didn't realize that this was a real possibility to her. And so she was exorcising her demons the only way she could.

And then I realized that my dad had always used humor to deal with uncomfortable situations. Many people had felt awkward around him because he was missing a leg, so he worked to make them comfortable. I told Rebecca every story about him that I could: about how he had used his artificial leg as an ashtray; how he would paint his wooden leg bronze every spring and then try to tan the rest of his body to match it; how he would gather the neighborhood kids around him, hammer a nail through his wooden knee, and tell them to go home and ask their dads to do the same thing.

I didn't say this to Rebecca, but I thought it would be less frightening for her if we could joke about it. And for me, it was the old "I whistle a happy tune and no one ever knows I'm afraid." I would start singing, to the tune of "Johnny Angel," "Ret-in-i-tis!" and she would sing back, "Pig-men-to-sa!" Or I'd pretend I didn't see a doorframe and bang my head on it, she'd do the same, and we'd fall on the ground laughing. "What's the matter, kid?" I'd shout. "Are you blind?"

I'm sure she's still frightened at times, but she doesn't show it. Just a year after she was diagnosed, she said matter-of-factly, "I'm not scared. If I go blind, I'll deal with it." And one time, when we were out for a walk, she looked up at the sky and said, "It's okay, Daddy, if I go blind, because I'll always have you and Mom with me to tell me what you see." How can you respond to that? You don't. You tuck it away and you wait till you're alone and then you deal with it. You just look at her and marvel.

From the beginning, Libby and I weren't sure if we should talk about Rebecca's disease publicly. But what struck a chord with

Rebecca was that we should campaign vigorously. She was very eloquent; she could describe not only her sight but her feelings. So we agreed that she would be a spokesperson. She even testified in front of Congress at age eight when we were trying to get funding to fight retinitis pigmentosa. Going public made sense to her; she felt she didn't need the help, but maybe there were other kids who did. Some would call that denial; others would call it spirit.

For the first seven months after she was diagnosed, I attempted to lose myself in my job, which marked my return to major league baseball after twenty years. But there was something missing. Baseball wasn't as much fun as I remembered, and I wasn't either. There was a sadness gnawing at my soul. And I couldn't work hard enough to forget how afraid I was. So finally, in May, I gave up the ghost and resigned from the Devil Rays.

I had devoted my entire life to the pursuit of this silly game. One day you're thinking, *I've got a dream job*. And a few days later, you'd trade anything or do anything. When I finally returned to the big leagues, I was like, *Yes, this is it*! And then to have it reduced to rubble and ashes in such short order is humbling. And you struggle; you have to rebuild your vision of yourself through the eyes of this wonderful child.

That's one of the things that all this has taught me—that what I laughingly call my career doesn't matter a pinch compared to what Rebecca's going through. And so she's become very inspirational to me. And because of that, I've been forced to learn more about this horrible disease. I never knew what "knowledge is power" really meant before—every time you learn a little more, the fear loosens its hold on you.

I took the next year to drive Rebecca around the country, and even fly her out of the country, so she could see all the things that had great swatches of colors that I had loved as a kid. I took her out of school to go see Death Valley and the Grand Canyon and

Pike's Peak. We drove down the Pacific Coast Highway and saw the giant sequoias. We went to Bermuda and Ireland. I took her to all the places that I thought would leave lasting, as Carrie Fisher calls them, "postcards from the edge." The goal was to go to all fifty states. Although she and I have a disagreement on the number, I think we have eighteen left to do. We had to slow down because both Rebecca and Libby reminded me that there was an attendance clause at school.

Rebecca wanted to see the home where I grew up, so I took her to the Eastern Shore of Maryland. It was tremendously emotional. Here I was, holding hands with my daughter and walking the paths that my father and I had walked.

She also wanted to see her grandfather's plaque in the Hall of Fame, so we went to Cooperstown, New York. There was a big gathering of my family, friends, and business partners that included Larry Doby and his wife, Helyn. My dad had signed Larry to be the first black player in the American League, eleven weeks after Jackie Robinson broke the color barrier with the Brooklyn Dodgers. One of my favorite photos is Larry picking Rebecca up that day so she could feel my dad's visage on his plaque. It was such a touching moment.

Well, I thought everything had been wrung out of me that could. But Rebecca delivered the absolute bomb when Jeff Idelson, a vice president of the Hall of Fame and a friend of ours, took us all downstairs into the catacombs where so many of the artifacts are stored. He had set out a picture of my dad and Larry Doby—a middle-aged white guy and a young black player. Rebecca looked down, and with perfect timing said, "Which one's grandfather?" And that brought down the house.

Over the years, Rebecca has resisted help every step of the way. She's fifteen now and is at blind camp this week. She went to her first camp at fourteen, and that was her first nod to the fact that she was different. She carries her collapsible cane surreptitiously in her backpack at school but tries not to use it. She has learned Braille because we forced her to, but she asks for no special treatment. She still has a sliver of sight left in one eye; she'll tell you that she can read everything but small print. She tells us, "I'll be fine. I'm a Veeck!"

I am blown away by her courage. It's awe-inspiring. You find yourself thinking, *Could I do that?* And the answer is always no. I look at it and think that it skipped a generation. She just has this indefatigable spirit, this tremendous bravery, and she absolutely refuses to be brought low by it. Just recently, Rebecca told us that she had had a dream years ago, before the doctor told her that she was going to go blind, in which a little girl, who looked like her but wasn't, came up to her, touched her eyes, and said, "I'm sorry, but you have a path to take."

In the long run, there could be a genetic-based cure for retinitis pigmentosa. Short-term breakthroughs have been made with microchips and miniature cameras. A dog named Lancelot had his vision restored with these implants. I live every day with this great hope that, while today may not be the day a cure is discovered, next year might be.

Yes, there can be any number of times in a day when you're drawn to tears, but she soldiers on so much that it would be betraying her to weep. I'm certainly not Pollyanna, but I don't feel that we're any more put upon than any other family in the world. We all have Rebeccas, every single one of us. I keep on reminding myself that there are autistic children out there and children who are dying, and I think, *Well, I don't have it so bad.* There are degrees of suffering, and it makes you acutely aware that Rebecca's condition is life-altering, but it isn't life-threatening.

And really, we're all one family—the family of man. We depend on one another. I depend on scientists to come up with a cure, they depend on Rebecca to raise funds and awareness, and in turn, people donate more money. It's very humbling, not only from the fact that you're helpless but that you have to rely on other people, and for the first time in my life, I take great comfort in that.

I've come to realize that there is nothing so unifying as watching a child struggle. It prioritizes your life. You become a different person. I'm not proud of the changes I had to go through, because I really did believe that being senior vice president of marketing for the Tampa Bay Devil Rays was very important. But then you realize that, thirteen seconds after you leave that job, nobody cares. And while I suffer fools easily because I am one, I am no longer able to see the loss of twenty season tickets as a failure of tragic proportions. It's so embarrassing to have been that egocentric.

Any parent who has to go through something like this is changed forever. I don't know what will happen when they discover a cure. Maybe you magically change back. I rather think not. I think you then look for something else to lose yourself in with another child who belongs to a friend or neighbor because it's so ingrained in you. All I know is that if Rebecca hadn't had this disease, I would now at fifty-six be the same person I was at forty-eight. I would be thinking, *It's all about me.* I don't think that way anymore.

21

DANNION BRINKLEY

Brinkley, who survived two lightning strikes, open-heart surgery, and brain surgery, which was followed by a grand mal seizure, wrote two bestselling books about his near-death experiences: Saved by the Light *and* At Peace in the Light. *In his third book,* The Secrets of the Light, *coauthored with his wife, Kathryn, Brinkley describes his third near-death experience and offers spiritual strategies for raising consciousness and empowering daily life. An early crusader for hospice and palliative care, Brinkley cofounded The Twilight Brigade, one of the largest end-of-life-care volunteer programs for dying veterans in American history. For more information, visit www.thetwilightbrigade.com and www.dannion.com.*

After I was struck by lightning in 1975, I endured twenty-eight minutes of clinical death, six days of total paralysis, seven months of partial paralysis, and two years of learning to walk and feed myself again. But in the end, the sacredness of the experience was overwhelming because I finally understood that we are great and powerful spiritual beings. Sacredness is found in the moment a person realizes who they are as part of the whole cosmic, divine universe, and I emphasize *divine*.

That near-death experience was a great blessing because, as I left my body and traveled down the tunnel, I came into a place of brilliant light and beheld the wonder of what awaits us all on our return home. The wonder of that experience inspired me to do what I could to help other people lose the fear of death.

I have the most beautiful wife and the most magnificent children—five girls and one boy—who a lot of times don't understand me because of my fixation and fascination with death. As soon as I hear someone's going to die, I light up like a Christmas tree because I know where that person is going, and I know the inherent beauty of the path home. For my wife and kids to be so tolerant of my hobby, which is death, I'm thankful to God for that.

I was with my mother when she passed in 1984. She trusted what I told her about the experience of going home, but she was still terrified. She said to me, "Don't let them hurt me anymore." She also said, "Take care of your father." I protected her and held her in my arms as she took her last breath and left this world.

I committed my life to those two things. The first—*Don't let them hurt me anymore*—is palliative care, or alleviating pain at the end of life without prolonging suffering. The second—*Take care of your father*—led me to begin taking him to the VA. He was a disabled World War II veteran, and I soon realized that a veteran is a unique person. I had served in the Marine Corps but had never gone through what I saw those guys going through. I combined these two passions by founding a nonprofit organization, The Twilight Brigade—also known as Compassion in Action—to recruit hospice volunteers for dying veterans.

We now have close to six thousand volunteers, and I'm so proud of them because they didn't have happen to them what happened to me. They have to have faith in me and in the way that I describe how life ends. I don't have to have faith in anything; I believe because I know—because I've been there.

One of the only places where you can take the word of God and put it to the test is when it's just you and that person preparing to leave this world. In that moment when the heavens open to receive their soul, and you have the privilege of being at that bedside, it's the most divine, sacred moment that anyone can have.

When you do it as often as I do it, you have moments with God that you find in no other situation.

My dad was really active until he was in his eighties, but he started getting really sick in 2004. He had an arrhythmia in his heart, and his lungs were giving out on him. He was a great guy—and tough, one of the hardest-working men ever. After he went into a coma, they put him on life support for thirteen days. The doctors told my brother, Jimmy, my sister, Becky, and me that our dad would probably not awaken from his coma, and that if he did, he would not be able to breathe on his own again. I looked at our dad lying there and said, "We can't leave him like this. This is nonsense. This is not our dad."

I went and found the doctor and said, "Please take my father off life support, turn him loose, let him go home." When the doctor pulled the last plug, my dad flatlined. My sister and I started to cry, my brother grabbed my sister, and we all held one another. Suddenly, my father woke up from the dead and said, "Do any of y'all have a job?" We just looked at him. We couldn't believe it. When we were kids working in my dad's grocery store, the three of us would often just stand around talking to each other. He'd walk up and say, "Do any of y'all have a job?" Because in the grocery business, there's always something to do.

As we all stood there incredulous, I realized what had happened. From my work as a hospice volunteer, I knew that sometimes dying people regain consciousness near the end. They literally return from the brink of death, and their loved ones think they're going to get well. But I know better; I've seen it too many times.

I went to get the doctor, and we moved Dad into a different room. That night he ate a full roast beef dinner, watched the Braves play baseball—his favorite pastime—and we made sure every family member we could find was there to enjoy his last moments. Dad held court that night. Around seven o'clock, he decided he needed to rest. He went to sleep but woke up hurting and struggling. He was so scared of passing, but my brother, sister, and I gathered around him and said, "Daddy, it's okay. It's time for you to go to the Light. We love you with all our hearts." He smiled, squeezed our hands, and said he had had the best day. He looked at us with a loving look, took two breaths, and headed down the tunnel.

We looked at each other with tears in our eyes and knew that we had just experienced one of the best days with our father that we'd ever known. The sacred sense of trust the three of us shared that day was incredibly powerful. We all knew we did the right thing, at the right time, in the right way. And most importantly, we did it together.

22

FRANCIS S. COLLINS, M.D., Ph.D.

Dr. Collins, one of the country's leading geneticists, is the author of the New York Times *bestseller,* The Language of God: A Scientist Presents Evidence for Belief. *Prior to moving to Washington, D.C., in 1993 to head up the Human Genome Project as director of the National Human Genome Research Institute, Dr. Collins helped to discover the genetic misspellings that cause cystic fibrosis, neurofibromatosis, and Huntington's disease. Working on the cutting edge of the study of DNA, the code of life, he has personally discovered some of the scientific evidence for the common descent of all living creatures. For more information, visit www.genome.gov.*

I had desired for some time to volunteer my medical services in a less developed part of the world. Finally, when I was thirty-nine, it came together because of the example and the encouragement of a physician who attended the same church that I did. He had been traveling to Nigeria and Ghana several times a year to set up clinics and offer medical care. The stories he told and the pictures he showed tapped into something in my heart that made me want to have that same experience and see what it was like.

I was particularly inspired to want to do this because my older daughter, by then a college student, was also thinking about medicine, and possibly medicine in other parts of the world. We decided it would be particularly rewarding if we did this together—maybe because we were both a little frightened by going to such an unfamiliar and politically unstable place.

So we agreed to go and serve in a small mission hospital in the Delta area of Nigeria, which was very economically depressed. My role would be to serve as a general internist, taking care of patients both in the outpatient clinic and in the hospital for a couple of weeks in order to give the full-time missionary physician time off to recharge his batteries and get some continuing education.

I expected the experience to be both exciting and daunting. I was aware that my medical skills, dependent as they were upon the high-tech world of an American hospital, might be poorly matched to the challenges of unfamiliar tropical diseases and little technical support.

Indeed, when I arrived there, I saw that the resources that I was so familiar with from my Western training were generally not available. There was not much in the way of a functioning laboratory. There was certainly no sophisticated imaging equipment, and the X-ray machine was often broken. At least the hospital had a pharmacy that had a reasonable collection of drugs that had a likelihood of providing benefit—if I could get the diagnosis right.

Ultimately, I found the experience rather discouraging. Most of the illnesses that I was asked to treat, such as tetanus, tuberculosis, malaria, and a wide variety of parasitic diseases, represented a devastating failure of a public health system that was utterly broken. There was no attention paid to cleanliness of water. There were no public services in terms of sewers or trash pickup. Vaccinations were generally not available. People had no access to basic preventive medical care, and many of them indulged in practices taught to them by witch doctors that were oftentimes the cause of illness rather than its prevention.

So I did what I could, seeing far more patients in a given day than I was used to, being rather uncertain in many instances about what their illnesses actually were, and trying to manage patients in the hospital without the kinds of medical support services I was used to.

And I began to wonder what on earth I was doing there. Before going to Nigeria, I had this image of myself as coming to save lives and help the whole country. Somehow my presence would make a difference. I would go back with exciting stories about how my efforts had made an impact on this part of the world. I began to conclude that I was a victim of a romantic and unrealistic vision and began to count the days until I could go.

I prayed about this because I had gone to this small hospital very much with a sense of calling, thinking that perhaps this was something that was supposed to be part of my life. I knew I had to lean more on God and less on myself because my own capabilities were insufficient to the task, and I felt quite disappointed that I didn't feel the joyful presence of the guidance that I had hoped for. I sank further and further into discouragement and no small dose of self-pity.

Four or five days went by. I took care of a myriad of problems, helping some patients, not knowing what to do with others, but generally having the sense that whatever I did was only putting a finger in the dike of what ultimately would be a disaster for most of these people. It was discouraging, knowing that many of them would go back to the same environment that had been the cause of their illness, only to be stricken by something else.

Then, a young farmer with a very puzzling illness was brought to the clinic by his family. In the previous couple of weeks, his legs had gradually swollen to twice their normal size. He was weak, almost unable to stand, and appeared very seriously ill. In examining him, I took his pulse, and a startling revelation was immediately apparent. His pulse, while palpable when he was breathing out, disappeared entirely when he took a breath in.

Though I had never observed this classic physical sign so dramatically demonstrated, I recalled that years before, as part of my medical training, I was taught that if someone's blood pressure goes down significantly when they take a breath in, that's something important to pay attention to. It's called a "paradoxical pulse." And I recalled, although I had to remind myself by quickly looking this up in my old medical manual, that this was usually an indication of fluid in the pericardial sac around the heart—a very dangerous condition. If the fluid builds up to a large extent, it keeps the heart from being able to relax, as it needs to do, between each heartbeat so that it can receive blood from the veins and then pump it out again. This all began to make sense because it explained why this young man's legs were so grossly swollen—the blood was pooling in his legs because his heart couldn't expand to receive it.

In the United States, that kind of suspicion would immediately be followed up by conducting an echocardiogram, where sound waves are bounced off of the heart to see whether there's actually fluid in the pericardial sac. Of course, there was no such instrument in this hospital in Eku, Nigeria. As it turned out, the X-ray machine was working that day, but the quality was quite poor; it showed that the heart shadow was larger than it should be, but it couldn't tell anything more specific.

I consulted with the other physicians at the hospital, most of whom were residents in training because most of the full-time doctors had gone off to a continuing education retreat. None of the other doctors in the hospital had ever carried out the procedure that would be needed, which would be the removal of the fluid through a needle.

I really felt in a terribly difficult spot. I wasn't absolutely sure of the diagnosis and could tell that this young man was severely ill and likely to go downhill quickly if nothing was done, yet I had never done this procedure myself. And I knew that the procedure had to be done under the most careful kind of guidance because a misplacement of the needle, and the nicking of the heart muscle itself, could be immediately fatal.

I read about the procedure and looked at some diagrams in the old books that were lying about in the hospital's library. And I pulled out my own manual of procedures that I had brought along to remind myself of how it was supposed to be done. The one thing I knew I could do that would be helpful was to be sure that all the equipment I had was sterile, so I made sure to have a completely sterilized syringe and needle. I hooked the needle up to an ancient electrocardiogram machine, because during the procedure, if you actually touch the heart, you will see a change in the electrical signal, and that will tell you to back off quickly.

This was a scary procedure. To be explicit, you place a large bore needle directly under the sternum, aim for the left shoulder, and advance the needle slowly, hoping to draw off the fluid around the heart and not the heart's blood, in which case you know you've gone too far and you may have just killed your patient. In the developed world, such a procedure would be done only by a highly trained interventional cardiologist, guided by an ultrasound machine.

The young man understood what I was doing and was remarkably peaceful about it. He knew the procedure was risky but urged me to proceed. And so, with my heart in my throat and a prayer on my lips, I inserted the needle just under his sternum and began advancing it. To my great distress, I saw the syringe fill with dark, red fluid. I was immediately concerned that I had gone too far, that my diagnosis was wrong, that I had essentially impaled this young man's heart.

But he seemed to be all right. I remembered that one of the conditions that would be most likely to cause his problem, namely tuberculosis, was capable of causing not just fluid around the heart but bloody fluid. So I squirted the fluid from the syringe into a pan and waited to see if it would clot. It did not. That meant it wasn't blood. Relieved, I continued to drain almost a quart of this fluid.

I removed the needle. Over the course of the next few hours I watched my patient carefully, hoping that I had not induced some bad outcome. In fact, his improvement was dramatic. His paradoxical pulse disappeared almost at once, and over the next twenty-four hours, the swelling of his legs rapidly improved.

So finally, after many days of feeling gloomy and disappointed in myself and in the whole Nigerian experience, I felt at least briefly exhilarated that something had happened here that was providing some benefit. But that feeling was short-lived. The next morning I woke up, again surrounded by the intensely needy environment of this hospital, feeling the oppressive equatorial heat, knowing there would be hundreds of patients for me to take care of that day.

With the same old weight of discouragement settling in on me again, I went about my daily rounds. After an hour or so, I came to the bedside of the young farmer. He was sitting up, looking surprisingly well, and reading his Bible. He spoke English quite well, as many in Nigeria do. I asked him how he was doing, and he described his situation in positive terms.

Then he looked at me quizzically and said, "I get the feeling that you're new around here." I was surprised by that. Maybe I should have explained to him just how new I was and that I basically had done a risky procedure on him that I really was not trained to do. I had not told him that, but he seemed to have figured it out anyway. That actually irritated me a little bit; I had wanted to come across as a very experienced, knowledgeable physician, and I didn't think it was so obvious that I wasn't. So, yes, I admitted that I had only been there a few days.

But he didn't stop there. He said, "You know, I get the sense that you are wondering why you came here." That really took me aback. *How did he know?* And then the words came out of his mouth that will stay with me for the rest of my life. He said, "I have an answer for you. You came here for one reason. *You came here for me.*"

I was speechless. Tears welled up in my eyes. I had the sense that while this was a young Nigerian farmer speaking to me—about as different from me in culture, experience, and ancestry as any two humans could be—it was really God speaking to me, reminding me that what life is all about is one person at a time trying to reach out and help somebody who needs it. I had plunged a needle close to his heart; his words directly impaled mine.

I had gotten completely carried away with a grandiose view of what my accomplishments in Nigeria were supposed to be. I had been driven by my own desire to feel important, by my own desire to do grand things that I could then go back and tell my colleagues about at the University of Michigan. I would then feel like I had accomplished something significant that affected lots of people, and my own reputation would be burnished as a consequence of telling those stories.

That young man's words reminded me that ego is the wrong motivation; it will never be satisfied or satisfying anyway. He taught me that what could be much more meaningful is the relationship between two human beings, connected in a way that could only make sense through the kind of love that requires no recompense, that is truly unconditional. That kind of love is one of the characteristics of human beings that we most hope to find within ourselves and most admire when we see it in others. And for just a moment there, that love settled over this young man and me in this unlikely place and reminded me what life is all about.

I had forgotten that the way in which you touch lives as a physician—or whatever your profession—is one person at a time in love, in benevolence, driven by an altruistic impulse. And that's enough; that's all that matters. It's all that has ever mattered. I learned that lesson in the most crystalline way in that moment, and that realization has stuck with me over the last eighteen years. It wells up now and then when I get a little carried away with some other grand mission or some new advance in what I now do, which is leading the Human Genome Project. I have to be pulled back from that and reminded that, just as that young Nigerian farmer taught me, we can really only change the world and spread God's love one person at a time.

23

SUZA FRANCINA

Suza, who prefers to be known by her first name, is a pioneer in the field of teaching yoga to seniors. She is the author of The New Yoga for People Over 50, Yoga and the Wisdom of Menopause, *and* The New Yoga for Healthy Aging. *She is a graduate of the Iyengar Yoga Institute of San Francisco, a certified Iyengar yoga instructor, and a member of the International Association of Yoga Therapists. A consultant for medical research studies on yoga, Suza teaches yoga internationally to people of all ages in a wide variety of settings. For more information, visit www.suzafrancina.com.*

I've always had an affinity for older people. When I was fourteen and living in Ojai, California, I began helping older people in our neighborhood with light household chores and errands. As I got older, I naturally fell in to taking care of them when they became ill. That's how I met Ruth, who had moved to Ojai to retire. I was doing home healthcare for her neighbors.

I began helping Ruth with her daily life chores when she was in her seventies. She was very healthy and vital. Like many of my clients, she became my friend. We would go for long walks together, and she'd share her insights with me. Ruth was an extraordinary person. She was a theosophist, a vegetarian, a lifelong student of esoteric and Eastern thought, and she would regularly meditate and fast. She was familiar with what I would call the ancient wisdom.

Fifteen years after Ruth and I first met, she had a stroke and began to lose control of her bowels and bladder. Her great fear was that she would have another stroke that would leave her mentally incapacitated.

Ruth and I had visited mutual older friends who had begun to deteriorate and had to be moved to a nursing home. The hallways were filled with people strapped to their wheelchairs. They were on multiple medications, they were completely out of their minds, and the opportunity to die gracefully was lost. Ruth was adamant that she did not want to go into a nursing home and lose her independence.

When one of Ruth's friends called and said that Ruth wanted to see me, I didn't think anything of it. When I walked into her apartment, her neighbor Betty, who was helping Ruth with her meals, was dumping oatmeal down the sink. She told me quite casually that Ruth was going to starve herself to death. Apparently, Ruth had had another stroke, was having memory lapses, and didn't want to wait so long that she couldn't make this decision.

Betty said that Ruth had considered this a few times before, and because she didn't want to become dependent, even fasted for a short while. The fact that she had lost control of her bowels and bladder was the last straw. She didn't like people having to come in and change her diaper.

When I went into Ruth's room, she was relaxing on her bed. I sat with her, and she explained to me that she was ready to stop eating and that she wanted to die at home. She asked me to be her advocate and make sure that nobody fed her. She chose me to be her guardian because she knew that I was aligned with her philosophy. I promised I would help.

Even though all this had taken me by surprise, after considering it, I felt it was a very wise decision. Ruth was accustomed to fasting for health and spiritual purposes, and that history would allow her to go through the process of letting go of her body by not eating or drinking. She had prepared for this the way I imagine that a holy person might.

Who knows? It may have been different if she had had family who would guarantee that they would never put her in a nursing home, or if she had the resources to hire people around the clock indefinitely. But she had never married and had no children. Add in the possibility of dementia, and it seemed like a sensible thing to do.

Ruth's physician also supported her. He was well acquainted with her philosophy and had agreed never to do anything to prolong her life against her wishes. His main concern was that she be kept comfortable.

Incidentally, while Ruth had been explaining everything to me, she took out her dentures, plopped them in a glass of water by her nightstand, and said, "I won't be needing these anymore." That gave us both a laugh. Right to the end, she would crack jokes like that.

Three days went by before I had time to visit Ruth again. She had enough resources to afford short-term, full-time care so there was always a home healthcare professional attending to her. Betty was over frequently as well. To the best of our knowledge, none of the paid workers realized that Ruth wasn't eating. Each of them must have assumed that the previous person must have fed her.

When I arrived, I saw that Betty had posted a giant sign on the refrigerator that read, "Ms. Smith does not wish to be disturbed. Do not offer food or water. Only if she asks for it." Ruth was happy to see me and was very pleased when I told her that she was definitely thinner.

I told Ruth that, in a few days, I would start spending the night with her, and that shortly after that, I would take off work in order to be with her full time the week before Christmas. But even as I made the promise, I doubted she would survive until then. Ruth was already so thin from a lifetime of frugal vegetarian living. I entertained the romantic notion that she'd take a pleasant leave of her body in just a few days. I envisioned myself holding her hand, her giving me one last smile and then exhaling and entering the great beyond, her spirit stoic and serene as it had always been. But real life isn't always like the movies.

Every day when I came, Ruth would be lying in the same position: on her back, with her head centered on her pillow in perfect alignment. In yoga, it's called savasana, the corpse pose. In a true savasana, you literally die to everything—to what you identify with, to all your worldly concerns. This practice of conscious relaxation, at a deeper level, takes you into what I call divine rest. It is a holy position.

I remember clearly when Ruth lost her voice. It was the fifth day. She had asked me to read to her from *Kim*, a novel by Rudyard Kipling. Since I'm from Holland and often pronounce things a little funny, she would always correct my pronunciation. Suddenly, I realized that she wasn't correcting me anymore. After that, she could only talk in a whisper.

We spent a lot of time in silence, just sitting. When you sit with someone who's dying, and you hold their hand, you start to tune in to the space that they're in. I felt like I was sitting in two worlds. When I'd leave her home and step outside, it was literally like stepping back into the stream of life.

I knew that I was observing something very sacred and profound. It's so unusual in our culture to be in the presence of somebody dying consciously. The body is the temple of the spirit, but it's also just a shell. Looking at Ruth, I could see that she was very much still there, but I began to sense that her life force was preparing to leave.

Right before I left one night, she motioned to me to come closer. Even with my ear right up to her lips I could barely hear her. "I'm so lucky to have friends like you," she whispered. She asked me to pull the covers up to her chin and then added, "You can leave anytime you want." We kissed good-bye several times.

"Good-bye, Ruth," I said. "I love you very much."

"And I love you," she replied.

Betty or I would walk Ruth to the shower almost every day. She was literally like a skeleton, like an apparition. I practically had to carry her into the shower. She would sit down on her walker and let the hot water pour over her. "Oh, the water feels so good," she'd say. "It feels so good to be clean."

Ruth had gotten rid of most of her worldly possessions. Her room was like a monastery, a sanctuary. It had no clutter; it was totally clean. We had all the windows open so she had fresh air. Every day we would bring fresh flowers. We made her room into a sacred space.

On the fourteenth day, as Ruth lay motionless, I took her bony hand in mine and asked her how she felt. She didn't say anything for a long time. Then she whispered, "I've looked forward to this for years." The way she said it was so transcendent, it brought tears to my eyes.

That night, Ruth's eyes became glassy and unfocused. But her heart continued its endless repetitions—the almost insane, mad task of pumping life force through her dying body. At midnight, she began to fidget. It was as if her spirit were fighting to fly out of her body. For some reason, I was gripped by fear. *Why can't her flesh release her spirit?* I wondered. *Why can't she relax and let go?*

On the sixteenth day, the night of the winter solstice, I was so exhausted that I needed to nap at home before driving over for the night shift. Betty had called earlier to tell me she had to leave by nine o'clock. When I woke up, it was past nine, and by the time my boyfriend, Paul, drove me over, I was half an hour late and still half asleep.

As I opened the door, I tried to assure myself that Ruth was asleep as usual and hadn't even noticed that she had been alone. But when I walked in, I saw that she wasn't in bed. I freaked out, thinking that my worst fear of someone "rescuing" Ruth and rushing her to the emergency room had come true. As I screamed for Paul, I saw that Ruth had fallen off the far side of her bed and was hanging face down, tangled up in her sheets. I felt terrible, especially because she may have been like that for half an hour. We put her back in bed, put a cold cloth over the bump on her forehead, and made her as comfortable as possible.

Before long, she began fidgeting again. I didn't know if she was in pain, but it was like her spirit was trying to wrestle out of her body. I said good-bye to her and left her alone with Paul. Like a labor coach, he held her hand and softly said, "Be at peace, Ruth, you are going somewhere beautiful." We checked on her every hour. Around 4 AM, I saw that she was turning yellow. I woke up Paul, and he turned on the overhead light. Her head was perfectly centered on the pillow. He checked her pulse and confirmed that she was gone.

Today, twenty years later, I am grateful to Ruth for providing me with a wonderful role model: she died with dignity and with all her faculties intact. Helping her die gave me a deep awareness of the inevitability of death and of the knowledge that everything is transient, everything changes. It brought me more in touch with the sacredness of life and death and how the two are connected.

Ruth exercised tremendous freedom and intelligence in choosing the way she left this world. Now that I'm older, I more fully understand how courageous she was. In this society, it's still very extraordinary to die like that.

My experience with Ruth also deepened my passion for teaching older people, which is very different from teaching younger students. You have to have more patience and go slower. I don't mind showing an older person how to practice a pose carefully, with props, because I know that yoga keeps them vital. I take great satisfaction in helping older people stay healthy and live independently for as long as possible. And yoga, which teaches us to live more comfortably in the body, also helps us let go when the time comes.

24

LARRY JULIAN

Julian, a successful consultant and speaker, specializes in biblically-based leadership development and strategic planning. He's authored two nationally acclaimed business books: God Is My CEO: Following God's Principles in a Bottom-Line World *and* God Is My Success: Transforming Adversity into Your Destiny. *Julian's mission is to help businesspeople integrate their work and faith to be the success God intended them to be. For more information, visit www.larryjulian.com.*

I have a strong faith, but a few years ago, I went through "a difficult walk in the desert." My wife and I were trying to have a child and had already experienced a miscarriage. I had also had five years of nothing but failures and discouragements in trying to get *God Is My CEO* written and published. I had wanted to quit a hundred times.

In November 1998, I got hit with a one-two punch that literally put me on my knees. I had gone to New York to shop the book to major publishers with my agent. When five publishers agreed to take part in a blind bid that Friday, I felt like all the frustrations were coming to an end and the book was finally going to be picked up. But by the end of the day, there were zero offers. I felt totally rejected and was ready to give up on the book once and for all. Then, a week later, on the heels of that first devastating blow, my wife had a second miscarriage. I was in tremendous emotional pain, and I asked God in great anguish why all this was happening.

A day or two later, I was sitting in a Caribou Coffee in Plymouth (Minnesota). A huge storm system was coming through, and it was raining heavily. Now, I love the weather; I've always been a weather fanatic. But that afternoon, when I was in great despair, I saw something I had never seen before. Without warning, the storm clouds parted, the rain stopped, and there was a patch of blue sky with a ray of sun shining down, as if there were a hole in the sky. In the midst of my personal storm, I was witnessing the eye of the storm, a very rare thing to see. It was almost as if the Lord was talking specifically to me, assuring me that everything was going to be okay. It was a very, very powerful experience, and I felt a tremendous peace come over me. It brought me to a much deeper place in my oneness with God.

Within the next couple days, at the very time when I needed comfort and support, two of the most important people in my life called and asked how I was doing. I saw clearly that all of this was a perfect illustration of how the Lord speaks to us through both circumstances and people.

This calls to mind a scripture, Romans 8:18: "I consider that our present sufferings are not worth comparing with the glory that will be revealed in us." I now know this to be true. Nothing is wasted. Suffering is important because suffering produces hope, and hope does not disappoint. As you suffer, not only do you grow closer to God in spirit, but you also become more valuable because you are then able to help others who are struggling. Now, as a speaker and author, I provide comfort to others who are hurting like I was. That's what God does; He helps us so we can help others.

Ten months later, I finally got a book contract. Ten months after that, our daughter, Grace, was born. Eight months later, in the spring of 2001, I took my daughter to the Ridgedale Mall just to walk around with her and give my wife a break from childcare.

My book was due to come out soon but I hadn't seen a copy yet. As we were walking by a B. Dalton bookstore, I looked over—and there was my book on display in the window. I'll never forget that moment. I remember thinking that God had a great sense of humor because the first time I set my eyes on my book was while walking with my daughter. It was like getting blessed with two miracles at once. That's what I love about the Lord; He always delivers on his promises.

25

CHRISTIANE NORTHRUP, M.D.

Dr. Northrup, an obstetrician/gynecologist, is an internationally known visionary in women's health and wellness. As a practicing physician for over twenty years and a former assistant clinical professor of obstetrics and gynecology (Ob/Gyn) at Maine Medical Center, Dr. Northrup is a leading proponent of medicine and healing that acknowledge the unity of the mind and body as well as the powerful role of the human spirit in creating health. Her books include Women's Bodies, Women's Wisdom, Mother-Daughter Wisdom, *and* The Wisdom of Menopause. *For more information, visit www.drnorthrup.com.*

I never intended to go to medical school. I wanted to be a biology teacher. I was also interested in music. In fact, I minored in applied music through the Cleveland Institute of Music's Harp Department. But, through a series of quirks, I ended up at Dartmouth Medical School in Hanover, New Hampshire. My experience has been that spirit is always leading me, even though my ego doesn't know in which direction.

Although I was in medical school, I figured I'd just do research and never actually practice. I had watched my aunt and uncle, who were both medical doctors, lead a life that I just wasn't interested in. They were on call constantly, they had to leave every Christmas and Thanksgiving dinner, and it looked like a lousy way to live.

Then we had our first Ob/Gyn rotation. When the other medical students and I gathered to watch our first delivery, I was so moved I began to cry—I thought I was going to fall down on the floor sobbing. Luckily, I had been in the culture of medicine long enough to know that I didn't want to be seen as a crying woman who loses it, especially when we were one of the first classes that included a significant number of women.

One of the medical students hadn't clamped the umbilical cord properly, and it became a mini fire hose, spurting blood all over the room. The nurse was yelling at the student, and another nurse was whisking the baby away. And every cell in my body cried out, *Why don't you people understand that this is a holy moment? How can you be yelling at this student? We should all be down on our knees in awe and reverence!*

Watching that birth was one of the holiest moments of my life. And I realized that being around women giving birth was as easy to me as breathing. I was drawn to that practice like a moth to a flame. In July 1975, I started my Ob/Gyn residency at Tufts New England Medical Center in Boston.

I chose Boston because my husband had been offered a place in the Tufts orthopedic residency. The previous September, we had decided to get married in May—a month before I'd get my M.D.— partly because we wanted to do our training in the same city; and we knew I had a better chance of getting a position myself if we could tell the chief of the Ob/Gyn program that we were married and wanted to be in the same area. This was back in the time when if you were going to be taken seriously in your profession, you couldn't say to the chief of the department, "Well, I want to be in this program because my boyfriend is going to be in this city and I want to be with him." That just wouldn't cut it. Our chances were better if we were married. It's no secret that the culture of medicine was not particularly supportive of one's personal life at that time.

I loved my training in Ob/Gyn. I really took the time to sit with my patients and listen to what was going on with their health and in their lives. When a woman would have a miscarriage in the middle of the night and I would be there taking care of her, I always knew that I needed to deal with her grief. This wasn't just a blighted ovum or a mistake of genes, this was the loss of a baby. It was a Catholic hospital and many of the women were Catholic, so sometimes we'd baptize the "products of conception," as we called them. These, too, would become holy moments. There was a constant sense of the sacredness of life running through my practice, but it was in a setting where this was never acknowledged and where it had to be kept hidden.

Fast-forward to 1985. I was completely burned out with my conventional practice. I had two little kids by then and decided I needed to work in a setting that supported what it means to be a woman and a mother. So three of my colleagues and I opened a center called Women to Women in Yarmouth, Maine. It was a model for what has now become very common: a women's center run by women. But it was a radical idea at the time. A male doctor actually said to me, "Oh, my God, you're going to have a center that sees women and is going to be run by women? Don't you think that's a little imbalanced?" Like, hello?

But it wasn't long before we realized that we were as exhausted as we ever were when the guys had been running the practice. We were working way too many hours and neglecting our own health. We also suspected that one of my colleagues had an addiction problem. I realized that we had met the enemy, and she was us. We had been determined to run our practice differently, but here we were, out of balance, burned out, and sick, wondering, *Why is this so hard?*

We couldn't figure out what to do, so the four of us signed up for a ten-day co-dependency intensive led by Anne Wilson Schaef, the author of *Women's Reality*. It was called the "Living in Process" seminar, and people just sat in a circle and talked about what was going on in their lives. Frequently, when someone would tell a particularly poignant story that moved them emotionally, they'd get down on a mattress and let their feelings arise. I felt like I was watching labor and birth again. These men and women would cry, wail, or pound the wall as long as they needed to. But I noticed that they would look younger and better when they got up and that they would also get healthier as time went on. Yet I was so well trained in Western medicine and left-brain thinking that I was able to watch all this very objectively. I wasn't thinking that any of it applied to me. I just thought, *Oh, you poor people, you've got so much pain.*

Then we did an intervention with my colleague. Now, the three parts of an intervention are as follows: first, you tell the person how much you love them and what they mean to you; second, you tell them how their behavior is impacting you; third, you tell them what the limits are and what will happen if they continue with their addiction. So we sat in a circle, and I told her how much I appreciated her for things like parking my car once when I was coming into the hospital; in the culture of medicine at that time, women were not very supportive of other women, and she had been supportive of me.

All of a sudden, I started to cry. In the witness part of my mind, I saw myself starting to have one of those processes that I'd been watching for eight days and taking pity on people for. So Anne said to me, "Do you want to get down and see what comes up?" I pushed back the tears, pulled myself up by my bootstraps, got it together, and said, "No, I think I can handle this." And Anne looked at me and said, "You are so tired." And then the dam broke, and I was down on that mat sobbing uncontrollably.

I was crying for all the times I never got to rest and for all the times I never got to be with my kids. After I got through all my stuff, I found myself crying for all the times my mother never rested and for the pain she had felt from losing two children. Then I was crying for my grandmother's pain of losing her mother when she was three. And then, when all that was done, I dropped into the place in the collective unconscious that I call "the pain of all women." And when I hit that, I started to make those sounds you hear in the Middle East at the Wailing Wall— primal sounds of pain. I didn't know that I had those sounds in my body. And as I continued, the whole room began to sob in the same way. I don't know how long it went on—an hour, maybe two—but when it was over, I knew exactly why I had gone into Ob/Gyn. I knew why I had been born. I knew why I was doing the work I was doing. It was to take this collective pain and transform it into joy. And I realized that the first birth I witnessed, which had moved me to tears, would have led me to this same place had I allowed myself to go all the way into the process.

There have been many, many moments of joy and laughter along the way, but I feel that now, after writing three books and going through menopause, the joy part is just beginning. And that excites me enormously.

26

RACHEL NAOMI REMEN, M.D.

Dr. Remen is Clinical Professor of Family and Community Medicine at the University of California San Francisco School of Medicine, a cofounder of the Commonweal Cancer Help Program, and the founder and director of the Institute for the Study of Health and Illness at Commonweal. She is an internationally known teacher and the author of the New York Times *bestsellers* Kitchen Table Wisdom *and* My Grandfather's Blessings. *Her course for medical students, "The Healer's Art," is currently being taught in fifty-three medical schools nationwide. For more information, visit www.rachelremen.com.*

When I was in my mid-forties, my mother, who was almost eighty-five, elected to have coronary bypass surgery. She had had recurrent episodes of pulmonary edema and had been rushed at night to the emergency room over and over again. The surgery was a heroic effort to try to gain a few more years for her, but it was high risk and ultimately unsuccessful.

After surgery, she was wheeled to the coronary intensive-care unit. For the first week, she was unconscious, peering over the edge of life, breathed by a ventilator. As I sat with her, I remember feeling awed by her will to live and by the capacity of the human body to endure such a massive insult at such an advanced age.

When she finally regained consciousness, she was profoundly disoriented and often did not know who I, her only child, was. The nurses were reassuring. They told me they saw this sort of thing often. They called it Intensive Care Psychosis and explained that, in an environment of beeping machines and constant artificial light, elderly people with no familiar cues often go adrift. Nonetheless, I was concerned. Not only did Mom not know me, she was also hallucinating. She saw things crawling on her bed and felt water running down her back.

Although she didn't seem to know my name, she spoke to me often and at length, mostly of the past and about her own mother, Rachel, who died before I was born. I had been named for her, although I was called by my middle name, Naomi. My mother and my uncles had always lovingly referred to their mother as a saint, saying that "No one needed to be homeless or hungry if they could make it to her back door."

She spoke of the many acts of kindness that her mother had done without ever realizing she was being kind. "Chesed," said my mother, using a Hebrew word that roughly translates as "lovingkindness." My grandmother's kindness was a central element of our family's story.

My mother also spoke of her mother's humility and great learning, of the poverty and difficulty of life in Russia, which she remembered from her childhood. She recalled the abuses and hatreds that the family suffered at the hands of the Russians and that, while many others had responded with anger, her mother had reacted only with compassion.

Days went by and my mother slowly improved physically, although her mental state continued to be uncertain. The nurses began correcting her when she mistook them for people from her past or pointed at the birds she saw flying and singing in her room. They encouraged me to correct her as well, telling me this was the only way she might return to what was real.

I remember one visit shortly before she left the intensive-care unit. I greeted her and asked if she knew who I was. "Yes," she said warmly, "you are my beloved child." Comforted, I turned to sit on the only chair in her room, but she stopped me. "Don't sit there," she said. Doubtfully, I looked at the chair again.

"Why not?" I asked.

"Rachel is sitting there," she said. I turned back to my mother. It was obvious that she quite clearly saw something I could not.

Despite the frown of the nurse who was adjusting my mother's IV, I went into the hall, brought back another chair and sat down on it. My mother looked at me and the empty chair, next to me with great tenderness. Calling me by my given first name for the first time, she introduced me to her visitor. "Rachel," she said, "this is Rachel."

My mother began to tell her mother about my childhood and how proud she was of the person I had become. I was very touched to hear this, as my mother had never spoken of it to me. My family had not been a family that openly offered much praise but, instead, encouraged one another to reach higher, to achieve more. I knew she was proud of my achievements. I had not known that she was proud of me as a person.

My mother's experience with my grandmother Rachel's presence was so convincing that I found myself wondering why I could not see her. It was more than a little unnerving. And very moving. Periodically, she would appear to listen and then would tell me of my grandmother's reactions to what she had told her. They spoke of people I had never met in the familiar way one does with gossip; they spoke of people like my great-grandfather David and his brothers, my great-granduncles, who were handsome men and great horsemen. "Devils," said my mother, laughing and nodding her head to the empty chair. She explained to her mother why she had given me her name, of her hope for my kindness of heart, and apologized for my father, who had insisted on calling me by my middle name, which had come from his side of our family.

Exhausted by all this conversation, my mother lay back on her pillows and closed her eyes briefly. When she opened them again, she smiled at me and the empty chair. "I'm so glad you are both here now," she said. "One of you will take me home." Then she closed her eyes again and drifted off to sleep. A few weeks later, it was my grandmother who took her Home.

Was my grandmother truly in that chair? I don't know. Such happenings can never be known or understood but only wondered about like the mysteries they are. Nonetheless, I feel grateful to have witnessed my mother in this way and to have been given something to wonder about for the rest of my life.

My mother's conversation with my grandmother seemed deeply comforting to her and became something I revisited again and again after she died, particularly her hope "for my kindness of heart." I was a professional, and I had not succeeded through "lovingkindness." I had been one of the few women in my class at medical school in the '50s and one of the few women on the faculty at the Stanford medical school in the '60s.

At that time, medicine was a very tough and male-dominated field that did not welcome women. The way to be treated as an equal in this male world was to become as macho as possible. The gentler human qualities were commonly regarded as a weakness in both men and women. Consequently, I had denied and repressed the feminine side of my nature. I succeeded in the way that most women succeeded in a man's profession in those days: by being very, very good at what I did, by being tougher and smarter and working much harder than most others.

I had dealt much the same way with my Crohn's disease, the debilitating and chronic illness that developed in my teen years. I struggled to master my body and overcome my physical limitations through stubbornness, discipline, self-absorption, courage, and a certain kind of fierceness.

Yet although I was expert at dealing with limitations and challenges of various sorts, after my mother's death, I slowly came to realize that despite my successes, I had perhaps lost something of importance. Over many years, I had been moving in the direction of a personal healing, piece by piece toward a reclaiming of my authentic self. When I turned fifty, I began asking people to call me Rachel, my real name.

27

PETER RUSSELL

Russell is a world-renowned futurist and fellow of the Institute of Noetic Sciences, a nonprofit membership organization that conducts and sponsors research into the nature of consciousness. He has authored eight books, including The Global Brain Awakens, The Consciousness Revolution, *and* From Science to God. *For more information, visit www.peterrussell.com.*

In April 2003, I was conducting a "Wisdom of the Dolphins" workshop in Hawaii. We were swimming with wild dolphins off the Kona coast each day. The last day we were there, many dolphins came down the coast in pods of five to eight, which tend to be the size of their family unit. The various pods all gathered together in a single group of about two hundred dolphins in a semicircular bay.

As we arrived in the bay, following slowly behind them, ten of them turned and jumped twice out of the water straight toward us at the bow of the boat. They then swam off and rejoined the others. All of them then settled into the bay. As we got into the water with them, they were still grouped in their family pods but were hardly swimming. They were almost static. The water was exceedingly clear. You could see a hundred feet straight down.

The dolphins then began slowly spiraling down beneath us. They weren't really swimming; they were just sort of sinking in slow spirals and eventually dropping out of sight. Five to ten minutes later, I looked down and thought I saw some fish. It took a few seconds to realize that these weren't tiny fish; they were the dolphins reappearing. They swelled up again in a spiral and floated up toward us. They took some air, and then they all went down again. This cycle went on six to eight times over a period of an hour or two.

Watching them was unexpectedly powerful and moving. I felt I was witness to some sacred dolphin space. The thought occurred to me that this bay might be their equivalent of a cathedral in the water. We humans build cathedrals as high places, where our minds can soar up into the heights where we imagine the angels are. But a dolphin's world is inverted. Much as human beings are tied to the ground, a dolphin is tied to the ocean's surface, which it has to keep making contact with for air. So, whereas we build cathedrals to enclose a great space and height, maybe this bay was a natural "structure" for the dolphins, enclosing a great depth.

And whereas with human beings, the question is, *How high can we fly?*, with dolphins it may be, *How deep can we sink?* There may be something sacred to them about sinking deep. Obviously, out in the ocean, they could go as deep as they'd like. But here, in the bay, they could go deep and be surrounded by a semicircle of land. That seemed to be important because, with their echolocation, they can "hear" the land around them.

They had come long distances to meet in this particular bay. They could have done what they were doing anywhere. The biologist's standard explanation would likely be, "They're just resting after a long night of fishing." But I don't think dolphins would travel twenty miles just to rest; they'd rest wherever they happened to be. I had a strong intuitive sense that they had gathered here as a group for a specific reason.

I wasn't the only one who felt this way. There were twelve of us in the water, and almost everyone had the same feeling, that we were witnessing a sacred dolphin experience. The stillness and peacefulness was very powerful and precious.

Adding to the sereneness of the moment was the song of the humpback whale in the background. A few of these whales were a couple miles away, and their beautiful moaning sound carries for great distances underwater. It struck me that, just as when we're out in nature and hear the songs of the birds, the dolphins were surrounded by the songs of the humpback whales.

Suddenly, I realized that I was a long, long way from the boat. I felt myself moving into a slight panicky mode because I'm not a strong swimmer. I had been caught in Hawaiian currents before and nearly drowned, so I'm very respectful of them. Trying not to panic, I started swimming back in the direction of the boat, which was now just a tiny speck on the water. I totally forgot about the dolphins. I was thinking, *I've got to get back toward safety, toward the boat.* Suddenly, the dolphins appeared again beneath me. They were spiraling back up.

I was amazed to find that all sense of fear and anxiety in me evaporated instantly. Often, when I'm recovering from that kind of fearful reaction, the anxiety gradually dies away. But in this instance, as soon as I saw the dolphins, the anxiety just switched off. One moment it was there, the next it was gone. I found myself turning around and swimming back out to sea, away from the boat, following the dolphins beneath me. The voice in my head was saying, *You're crazy! You're a long way from the boat and security, and you know how dangerous these currents are. What are you doing swimming out to sea with the dolphins, away from safety?* But I knew deep inside that I was totally safe, that everything was absolutely okay. I found that instant shift in consciousness quite fascinating. I swam with the dolphins for a while longer, and needless to say, I did make it back safely.

When it was time to leave, when we all climbed back into the boat and started it up, the dolphins again stopped what they were doing, swam over to the boat, leapt around it, and then followed us out a ways. They had been aware of our presence the whole time. They both welcomed us into their ceremony and acknowledged our departure. And that's what it had felt like: like we were witnessing some spiritual ceremony performed by another species. That's the only way I can describe it. It was a very magical experience and one that had a deep impact on me afterwards.

I've swum with wild dolphins a number of times, and I've noticed that, in the days afterward, I'm changed. This time, two days later, I was giving a lecture, and I noticed myself feeling a very different sense of freedom as I spoke. In fact, I gave four lectures over the next week that all had a very different feel to them. I felt very spontaneous, very alive, and very supported in some way. I had this sense that the peace and sacredness of my time with the dolphins had stayed with me.

28

DAVID WAGNER

Wagner, an internationally acclaimed hairstylist, entrepreneur, and "Daymaker," is the owner of Juut Salonspas, the original Aveda salons. His bestselling book, Life as a Daymaker: How to Change the World Simply by Making Someone's Day, *is generating a worldwide kindness movement. Wagner has worked with the U.S. Navy on Project Daymaker, a program designed to increase retention of enlistees. For more information, visit www.daymaker movement.com.*

Back in 1986, I was traveling around the country performing at hairstyling shows for Aveda. At a show in Dallas, I was cutting hair and bantering with the audience. I remember saying, "Imagine if we brought the intention of making our clients' day to work every day, how much fun we'd have." I hadn't planned to say that; it was completely spontaneous.

That night, on the flight home, I sat next to a very conservative businessman in first class. There I was with my big rock 'n' roll hair and leather pants. I looked like the lead singer from REO Speedwagon. This businessman looked at me and asked, "What do you do?"

I said, "I'm a Daymaker."

"You're a what?" he asked.

I said, "I'm a Daymaker."

He said, "What in the world is a Daymaker?"

I said, "I make people's day."

That's how I coined the term—it just came out in the conversation. I liked it so much that I tossed out my business cards the next day and ordered new ones with "Daymaker" under my name instead of "Stylist." I started passing them out to customers and prospects, and people really got a kick out of it. So that's how it started out, as a lark.

Six months later, I was working in my salon when a regular customer came in to get her hair styled. I was surprised to see her since it was right in the middle of her five-week period between haircuts. I figured she must have an important social engagement that evening since she asked for her hair to be styled instead of just cut. "No, I don't have anything special going on," she told me. "I just want to look and feel good tonight."

Luckily, I was able to fit her in. I was in a great mood that day and I was really "on." I gave her a great scalp massage and shampoo like I always did and then styled her hair. We had a blast the whole time. We laughed and joked and entertained each other. When she left, she gave me a big hug that lasted just a little bit longer than usual.

Two days later, I got a letter from her. When I started reading it, I froze. She said she had planned to commit suicide that day, and she had come in to get her hair styled so it would look good for her funeral. She said that she had changed her mind during her appointment, that I had helped her realize that her life could be better. She had gone home and called her sister to tell her what she was going through, and her sister had taken her to the hospital.

I was stunned. If you had lined up a hundred of my clients and asked me to choose the one who was considering taking her own life, she would have been at the end of the list. She was gregarious, she was outgoing, and she seemed successful. I had no idea that she was in such a dark place. I was glad, and humbled, to have made such a difference, yet I also felt a little uneasy.

I wondered what would have happened had I been upset or distracted when she had come in and I had just gone through the motions of cutting her hair.

That day, I began to feel an enormous sense of responsibility. How many of the ten to fifteen clients I saw every day might be in a personal crisis and in need of a little extra kindness and attention? Even if it was just one person a week, I realized what a big difference I could make. I resolved then and there to treat every customer like I had treated that woman.

Today, whenever I catch myself thinking only of my own agenda, I go back to the moment when I opened that letter. And I remind myself that days are made of moments, and how I choose to be in those moments is what's going to determine the quality of my day, which in turn can affect the quality of someone else's day. What it all comes down to is this: If you're going to be there, be there. You might be somebody's only angel of the day, and you can't take that for granted.

Part III

INSIGHTFUL INCIDENTS

*The universe is full of magical things patiently
waiting for our wits to grow sharper.*
Eden Phillpotts

Ordinary moments can lead to extraordinary insights.
Something within you inexplicably shifts, and you view a
chance meeting, a casual conversation, or a familiar ritual with
fresh eyes. The proverbial light bulb goes off, everything clicks
into place, and life makes more sense.

Growth is a cumulative force. Each new experience, each new
bit of knowledge adds another brick to the bridge between our
conscious mind and the collective unconsciousness. Eventually,
critical mass is achieved—the stars align, and we are presented
with opportunities to take the next step in our evolution.

"Insightful Incidents" is divided into two parts. "Life-Altering
Moments" includes stories of dreams, encounters, and synchronici-
ties that lead to transformation and course corrections. The
epiphanies recounted in "Moments of Enlightenment" spur deeper
appreciation and understanding of life's meaning and purpose.

Life-Altering Moments

29

MARILYN DIAMOND

Author of six books and an internationally renowned pioneer in enlightened living, Marilyn Diamond is coauthor of Fit for Life, *the revolutionary diet book that, at the time, became the bestselling diet and health book ever written. It cracked the list of the top twenty-five bestselling books in history and has since sold millions of copies in thirty-eight languages. Marilyn and husband Donald Schnell later wrote* Fitonics for Life *as a lifestyle sequel to* Fit for Life. *Marilyn can be reached at leelananda@aol.com.*

Donald and I were spending our tenth year of marriage in southwest Florida in the picturesque community of Old Naples. It had been our plan to live there for many years, and sure enough, when the time came, we were blessed to find our beach retreat only a few steps from the sand. I delighted in going out at dawn every morning for my walk along the water. My day was always inspired by the brilliant canvas of colors the sunrise painted in the sky over the aquamarine Gulf of Mexico.

On my fifty-seventh birthday, I strolled down the walkway between two magnificent beachfront estates. Their lush, tropical gardens and lawns seemed in full celebration beside me as I made my way toward the sand. The royal palms and poinciana dripping with coral blossoms reaching out to crystal white sand were a heavenly vision. I felt intoxicated by the sweet scents of tropical flowers and salty sea mist and the caress of the warm wind on my skin. Feeling overwhelmed with the sheer ecstasy of being alive, I slipped off my sandals and flung my arms upward in gratitude.

My bare feet kicked up powdery puffs of warm sand as I made my way to the water's edge. I stopped to watch a mountain of white clouds turn pink on the horizon as the radiant dawn light began to flood the sky. The lapping of the water at my feet sounded like laughter. Suddenly, right in front of me, a little pearl crab danced out of the shallow waves and headed up onto the shore.

The beach in that area was dotted with small mounds that the crabs had produced when they emerged from the water and burrowed into the sand to protect themselves from seagulls. I sensed the tiny crab was on that sort of mission, so I stopped in my tracks, not wanting to scare her. She froze and looked up at me.

I gazed back at the hexagonal, pearly-white face and jet-black eyes. Her multiple legs fell like golden locks of hair from behind her head. She stood statue-like, on tiptoes like a ballerina. I was riveted by this little being in front of me, who was clearly riveted by me. There we were, tiny crab and I. She was so incredibly small and delicate, and I felt her fear. Welling up from my heart was a profound compassion I'd seldom known before.

"Oh, beautiful one," I heard my words coming softly, "I would never hurt you; I could never hurt you."

Very slowly, she crossed her two front legs and sat down in the sand. I was spellbound. She was so astonishingly beautiful, such a perfect creation. The regal way she settled herself in front of me made me feel like the Goddess of the Sea was granting me an audience. My heart melted as a rush of precious memories flooded over me.

I recalled my grandma Ida's yearly visits to my home when I was a little girl. She would slip on her bibbed apron and bake huge apple pies that stood six inches high. She was always willing to listen to my problems and heal my little hurts and confusions. She would hold me on her lap so lovingly, and sometimes I would cry pent-up tears into her cinnamon-scented apron.

I remembered holding my three babies in the same tender way, and how wonderful it felt to kiss their little pink cheeks and put their tiny toes up against my lips. I thought of the grandchild who was soon to be born and practically swooned at how good it felt to be me.

Finally, I saw myself at my wedding to Donald in a rose garden in Santa Fe. While the elderly rabbi spoke to us of our eternal love and the cantor intoned the sacred Hebrew blessings, the husband I'd seen in my dreams as a child sobbed, and I sobbed with him. We were so indescribably happy. Our faces were wet with tears when we kissed, and our mouths were salty.

The wondrous blessings of life washed over me as I stood there in front of my little Mistress of the Sea. I sensed that she was my teacher and I was her disciple. That moment marked the birth of a powerful awareness in me.

It was the experience of ahimsa—the philosophy of nonviolence and non-cruelty that is the foundation of every major world religion. I think of ahimsa as a personal tribute to the passionate desire of all living beings to be free to go on living. In my heart of hearts, I knew I could never again tacitly tolerate the hurting of another living soul. This feeling set in motion a powerful awareness that nonviolence, universally practiced as the religions intended, could end suffering in the world. And it strongly awakened a goddess voice within me that whispered to the wind to carry the message to all humanity that we must honor the gift of life. All of us everywhere have the divine birthright to live in health, happiness, and peace.

I was in love with this tiny pearl crab, and I believe she was in love with me. We were sharing the breathless experience of loving life together. At that very moment, the huge golden orb of the sun rose up behind the trees, bathing us both in a sacred warmth, a celestial golden light. I felt us worshipping as one heart, one love, one being.

The cherished moment when a graceful creature of the sea transmitted to me the ancient wisdom of ahimsa will always be with me. It was after that morning that I began to write and speak about the relevance of nonviolence in daily life. After all, the Kingdom of Heaven is within all of us, and we reap what we sow. When we make the choice to inflict suffering on others, we create suffering for ourselves.

That unforgettable encounter with a tiny crab dramatically shifted my views on the practical steps we can take as individuals to heal the condition of our world. From that day on, I began practicing nonviolence and non-cruelty as guidelines for conscious living. The love and success this simple spiritual practice has brought to my life are the most powerful rewards I've ever known.

30

JEAN HOUSTON, Ph.D.

Houston, an internationally known philosopher, cultural historian, seminar leader, and educator, has worked and lectured in more than one hundred countries. Her twenty-six books include Jump Time, A Passion for the Possible, *and* A Mythic Life. *Drawing on her many years of work as an expert in human and cultural development, Houston, a protégée of the late anthropologist Margaret Mead, continues to develop revolutionary ways of unlocking the latent capabilities existent in every human being. She is the founder of the field of social artistry, which focuses on human development in the light of social complexity. For more information, visit www.jeanhouston.org.*

My father, Jack Houston, an agnostic Baptist and a descendent of Sam Houston of Texas, wanted to marry my mother, Maria Annuciata Serafina, a Catholic born in Siracusa, Sicily. So dad had to go to religious instruction school, taught by a young priest at Saint Patrick's Cathedral in New York. He and the priest traded jokes instead of theology, and finally the priest said, "Oh, Jack, you're just a natural-born pagan. Here, I'm going to give you a learner's permit so you can become a Catholic. But if any children come along, you have to bring them up Catholic and send them to Catholic school."

My father said, "Oh, yeah, sure, sure, I just want to get married."

Well, I, in due course, came along. The year that I was five, my father, a comedy writer, was thrown off the Bob Hope show for what was referred to as "an excess of high spirits," meaning he probably played some practical joke on Hope, and he was sent away for a year or so. With my father out of work, we soon found ourselves living with my mother's parents in the Sicilian section of Brooklyn—or Brookalina, as my grandmother referred to it.

Since my father had promised to send me to a Catholic school, I went to Saint Ephraim's in Brooklyn. Everything was fine except that my father would "gag up" my catechism and give me the most interesting questions to ask the poor little nun in the morning, such as, "Sister Theresa, I counted my ribs and I counted Joey Mangiabella's ribs, and we've got the same number of ribs. And I wonder, if God created Eve out of Adam's ribs, how come we all have the same number of ribs?" Before the startled nun could respond, I added, "I'll prove it! One, two, three, go!" And right on cue, thirty little children lifted their undershirts.

Then there were the Jesus questions: "Sister Theresa, how do you know that Jesus wasn't walking on rocks below the surface when he seemed to be walking on water?"; "Sister Theresa, when Jesus rose, was that because God filled him full of helium?"; and then finally, one day, the great question, the one that is in the mind of every little Catholic child at one time or another. This was such a great question, I checked it out beforehand with Denise Canzineri, who said, "Yeah, I've been wondering about that," and Joey Mangiabella, who said, "Yeah, you've gotta ask that."

Well, the mother superior was in the room that day. I raised my hand, and Sister Theresa, who by the way lisped a great deal, said, "Yesh?"

I said, "Sister Theresa"—I looked around and everyone was encouraging me—"did Jesus ever have to go to the bathroom?" Well, that did it.

The mother superior went flying out of the room. And Sister Theresa, in this huge torrent of rage, leaped up and yelled in her lisping fashion, "Blashphemy, blashphemy! Sacrilish and blashphemy!" She strode over to her desk, pulled out a sheet of oak peg, tacked it up on the wall, and in India ink, wrote in big letters, JEAN HOUSTON'S YEARS IN PURGATORY. From then on, every time I asked a question I shouldn't have, I'd hear, "Blashphemy, blashphemy!" and she'd mark a big X on the board. Each X equaled one hundred thousand years. At the end of first grade, when I turned six, she added it all up: three hundred million years in purgatory.

I went home sobbing. There was my father, typing away on his jokes. "What's the matter, kiddo?" he asked me.

I said, "Daddy, I have to go to purgatory for three hundred million years and it's all your fault." And he began to howl with laughter.

He picked me up, put me on his shoulder, made the sound of a choo-choo train with his feet, and went, "Purgatory, purgatory, purgatory, purgatory, toot, toot! Make way for the purgatory special!" He ran downstairs, out into the street, and past our Sicilian neighbors, shouting, "Purgatory, purgatory, purgatory, purgatory, toot, toot!"

The neighbors threw open their windows and called out, "Eh, there goes that Crazy Jack," and yelled out some choice words in Sicilian.

I asked, "Where are we going, Daddy?"

He said, "To the movies, kiddo. You think you have problems? Ha! Wait till you see what they did to a real saint, wait till you see how they hogtied poor old Bernadette." So we continued on to the Fortway Theater in Brooklyn, where *The Song of Bernadette* was playing. We sat down next to an old lady who had a chest full of holy medals. The picture began, and every time Jennifer Jones as Bernadette showed up, the lady next to us would cross herself and sigh in Sicilian, "Oh, what a beautiful saint!"

When the Virgin Mary shows up in a vision—one of the great spiritual scenes in the motion picture—the poor old lady next to me kept crossing herself and exclaiming in Sicilian. Suddenly, a horrible, mule-like whinnying laugh began to fill the theater. It went on and on. And it was coming from my father, who was in complete hysterics. "Daddy, shhh, this is the holy part," I said. But he was hysterical; he could barely talk to me, and people kept turning around and making evil Sicilian gestures at him. The lady next to us kept muttering, "Diablo, diablo!"

I shushed him again, and he said, through his guffaws, "You know who that is up there on the screen playing the Virgin Mary? Linda. We met her last year at that party in Beverly Hills. Linda, Linda Darnell. Hot dog, I told her she'd go far!" He found the incongruity between her Hollywood life and the role she was playing absolutely hilarious.

He couldn't stop laughing, so I pleaded, "Daddy, go to the bathroom; get out of here." He went stumbling up the aisle, still in hysterics. When he came back, he was pretty well behaved, expect for a few occasional snorts.

Going home from the theater, I was heady with purpose. As soon as we got home, I started walking purposefully toward the front door, and my father said, "Hey, kiddo, are you mad at me?"

"Yes," I said.

He asked, "Well, where are you going?"

I said, "Daddy, I don't want to tell you where I'm going because you'll laugh at me."

"No, no, I promise," he said.

"Oh, yes, Daddy, you will," I said. "You can't help yourself."

"No, no, I promise," he said again. "Where are you going?"

With great pride, I said, "I'm going to see the Virgin Mary."

"You are?" he said. "Hey, that's a great idea. I'll go with you!" He grabbed me by the hand and began to skip down the street

with me, singing a horrible song, which I will never forget—
"We're off to see the Virgin, the wonderful Virgin of Lourdes!
We'll join the hordes and hordes and hordes, the hordes to see the
wonderful Virgin of Lourdes!"

Appalled, I told him, "Daddy, go away, and don't you follow
me! This is the most important thing I have ever done in my
entire life."

I ran back home and up to the second floor, where we had a
guest room with a very deep closet. There were no clothes in the
closet because Chickie, my dog, had staked it out as a sort of
dog nursery, and she was lying there nursing her nine puppies.
I moved the puppies out into the room and said, "Chickie, you can't
be here. I'm sorry, but I don't want the Virgin Mary to step on you."
I got on my knees, crossed myself, and I looked at the walls, thinking, *Boy, this looks just like a grotto*. And I began to pray: "Virgin
Mary, please, please, please show up in the closet, just like you did
before Bernadette in Lourdes. If you do, I'll give up candy for a
week. No, two weeks, okay? Now I'm going to close my eyes and
I'll count to ten. And when I open them, you be there, okay? Okay."

I closed my eyes, counted to ten, and opened them. No Virgin
Mary. Instead, Chickie was bringing one of her puppies back into
the "grotto." I crossed myself again and said, "Virgin Mary, this
time I'll give up my favorite food—chicken with lemon and garlic
sauce and stuffed artichokes—and I'm going to count to twenty-
nine, and you be there, okay? Okay." I closed my eyes, counted to
twenty-nine, opened my eyes, no Virgin Mary—but Chickie had
brought two more pups back into the closet.

I began to count higher and higher numbers. And I gave up
everything. I mean, I gave up all sugar. I gave up all fats. I gave
up everything except broccoli, which I hated. Finally, I said,
"Virgin Mary, maybe you just don't know where I live. It's 1404
Avenue O, and Denise Canzineri is jumping rope downstairs.

I think you've got to cross the Brooklyn Bridge and go left. And I so much want to see you and I don't know what else to give up. Please, please come. This time, I'll count to 167, and you be there, okay? Okay." I closed my eyes and counted very slowly to 167, actually seeing her in my mind's eye, flapping across the Brooklyn Bridge and turning left toward my house.

I opened my eyes, certain she'd be there. No Virgin Mary. But there was Chickie contentedly licking all nine of her puppies. Giving up, I left the closet and walked over to the bay window. I just sat there, totally empty, in a dreamlike state. I looked down and saw my grandfather, Prospero Todaro, bending over trying to light the scrub pot by the fig tree in our front yard. I looked up and saw a plane flying across the sky.

And then, it happened. I must have, in my innocence, unwittingly tapped into the appropriate spiritual doorway, for suddenly, the key turned and the door to the universe opened. Now, it wasn't dramatic in any visual or auditory way. I didn't see or hear anything differently. All I can say is that suddenly everything opened up, and the whole world moved into meaning. Literally, all of reality was there, and it was all very good and interrelated and moving together—the fig tree in the yard, Chickie and her pups, the plane in the sky, the sky itself, my little Mary Jane shoes, my chewed-up red pencil, my grandfather's huge stomach, the little boy fishing in the lake who waved to me during a train ride across Kansas, the chipped paint on the ceiling, the silky ears of corn in a Texas cornfield, and all the music that ever was—all were in a state of resonance and ecstatic kinship. And I knew absolutely that I was an important part of this process. In the midst of this epiphany, I heard my father enter the house downstairs, laughing. Immediately, the entire universe joined in and began laughing— field mice tittered, and so did angels and rainbows—everything was laughing together in an extraordinary spiral of joy.

Years later, when I read *The Divine Comedy*, I remember Dante's description of his great vision in paradise: "d'el riso del universo"—*the joy that spins the universe*. That's what it was like, this incredible laughing, this joyous unity, this great connectivity of everything with everything else, this universal fellowship, and this perfect, glorious feeling of love. It was knowledge of the way everything worked—through love and joy and the utter union of everything with All That Is.

This experience has remained with me all my life. It was so very deep that it's influenced everything I've tried to do and everything I've tried to be. It was alive throughout my childhood and adolescence, this state of passion. I may have almost lost it for a while because I got a little bit overeducated. But whenever I lose touch with it, it always comes back. It was the single most luminous, most important experience of my life.

31

ROBERT IBRAHIM JAFFE, M.D.

Dr. Jaffe is the president and spiritual director of the University of Spiritual Healing and Sufism. He founded the university to deliver his comprehensive synthesis of medical, energetic, and spiritual healing to professionals and laypeople who want to heal in a complete and holy way. Dr. Jaffe, a master healer, teacher, and spiritual guide, also founded the Shadhiliyya Sufi Center in Napa Valley, California. He is a Sufi al-Murrabi a-Ruhi, a leader of the highest rank within the Shadhiliyya Sufi order, and he has dedicated his life to creating world peace through bringing people into the reality of divine love and healing. For more information, visit www.drjaf femd.com and www.sufiuniversity.org.

I was studying in an ashram in India in 1983 when I received word that I had been accepted to the University of Illinois Medical School. I began medical school there as an Indian sannyasin, the equivalent of a monk or other spiritual renunciant. I found out pretty quickly that the doctors and nurses there didn't like having a guy running around the hospital in orange robes. Fortunately, as the year went on, people got to know me, and they got over it.

My medical school training was unusual because I wasn't just learning medicine. I was also learning clairvoyant healing and the chakra energetics of disease. Once I had a diagnosis, I would look psychically at a patient's energy field and feel their chakras. I'd think, *Wow, so this is what the energetics of an atopic pregnancy look like*, or *This is what happens in the chakras during kidney failure*. I was particularly fascinated in following what happened to people's chakra systems as their days on earth drew to a close.

Toward the end of my first year in residency, I was transferred to the ICU for six weeks. For doctors, the ICU is the most sophisticated and challenging part of a hospital. You need a deep understanding of the technology of disease in order to make sense of all the lines and monitors that are hooked up to people and figure out what's going on inside of them. Also, everything happens quickly—you're perpetually dealing with code blues and cardiac arrests. It's a very intense place, in that you have to deal constantly with death.

One of the patients was a senior at an Orthodox Jewish high school in Chicago. She had a very rare form of chronic aggressive hepatitis and was dying from liver failure. When I saw her on her third day in the ICU, she was in a coma and her whole body was swollen up like a dead fish. Her heart was beating, and she was making jerky, spasmodic movements in her comatose state, but that was about it.

I went to feel her chakras because I wanted to get a sense of what was going on energetically with her. But as soon as I put my hand over her body, the energy that came out of her was so powerful that my hand went into a full-out cramp and my fingers spasmed into a claw. It was so agonizingly painful that I had to literally rip my hand off her body. It took three or four minutes before whatever came out of her was released from my hand. I had never dealt with such an intense energy of illness. In the days that followed, I was careful to avoid touching her body. When I'd examine her with my stethoscope, I'd drop the stethoscope onto her chest instead of placing it there with my hand.

She continued to spiral downward until she reached a point where we knew she only had a few days left. Her vital signs were out of control. Her pulse, which should have been about 80, was 150. Her respirations, which should have been around 12, were up around 40 to 50. Her temperature was hypothermic, around 94 to 96. And her blood pressure, which normally should have been at 120 over 80, was down to 50 over zero, barely enough to sustain life.

As she neared death, three Orthodox rabbis who had been regularly visiting her decided to consult with a head rabbi in Jerusalem. The head rabbi found a passage in the Talmud which said that the way to heal yellow hepatitis is to clean the feathers around a dove's sexual orifice and then place the dove over the belly button of the person with hepatitis. The passage said that if the dove dies, it means it's absorbing the disease and to continue to put doves over the belly button until they stop dying. At that point, the disease has been absorbed and the person may be healed.

One of the rabbis asked the chief of medicine whether he would allow doves to be brought into the ICU so that the girl could potentially be healed. The chief of medicine, who was also Jewish and who was very sad about losing this young girl, agreed. So the rabbis went around to pet stores and soon came in with a giant cage filled with around thirty doves. They said special prayers, cleaned off the orifice on a really big dove, and held it over the girl's belly button.

The dove took one breath and fell over dead. It was shocking. It was clear that something mysterious was at work. One after another, the doves kept falling over dead, with each one taking a little bit longer to die. The first dove lasted one second, the second one lasted maybe ten seconds, and the third one about a minute.

It was so amazing that I got a bit suspicious, thinking that the rabbi holding the dove may have been doing something to it that I couldn't see. I asked if I could hold a dove over the girl, but I was told, "No, you aren't a rabbi, so you don't have the permission of God to do this type of healing." I told them I was a sannyasin, but they said, "No, only as a rabbi will we accept this form of healing from you."

So I said, "Then can I put my hands over your hands so I can feel what happens?" They agreed to that, so as they were holding the dove over the girl, I put my hands over the rabbi's hands. All he was doing to the dove was holding it. He clearly wasn't squeezing it, pushing it down, or killing it in any way. The doves were dying purely from the energetic release of what was coming out of the girl's body.

This went on for three or four hours. They had gone through eighteen of the doves when the chief of medicine abruptly entered the room and told the rabbis they had to leave. Apparently what happened is that most of the doctors in the hospital came together, confronted the chief of medicine, and told him that if he didn't get the doves out of the ICU, where they could be spreading disease, they were going to have his license revoked. And he caved. You'd think the idea of bringing in a bunch of doves to heal a patient would have been interesting, or at least humorous, to the other doctors and residents, but it was just the opposite. I was shocked at their level of hostility.

The rabbis didn't protest at all. It was the strangest thing. Their heads were down, they picked up the cage, and they left. They didn't say anything; there was no fight. They just got up and walked out of the hospital.

After the rabbis left, I noticed a definite change in the girl's coloring. The yellowness had lessened significantly and so had her swelling. She almost looked healthy again. I checked her vital signs and they had all normalized. It was an incredible shift.

But that night, a few hours later, the girl's heart stopped. We did some CPR, and that was the end of it. I really believe that if the rabbis had been given a chance to go on, she would have been healed.

That was a defining moment for me in medicine because it deepened my interest in energetic healing. I saw with my own eyes that girl getting better as the energy of the disease left her body and killed those birds. I thought, *Whatever this type of healing is, that's what I want to learn.* I decided that night to end my family practice residency and fully dedicate myself to exploring alternative methods of healing. A few weeks later, at the end of my first year in residency, I took my exams to get my M.D.

Ironically, while the doves were not allowed to save that young girl's life, they did, in an indirect way, save mine, physically and spiritually, a dozen years later. As I mentioned, the incident with the rabbis had completely altered my healing path. Instead of pursuing a career as a cardiologist or family practitioner, I ended up establishing an integrative medical institute in Sedona, Arizona. I assessed my patients through a blend of traditional allopathic medicine and auric diagnosis, which involved clairvoyantly scanning their etheric, emotional, and mental bodies.

It seems like each patient I healed sent two more people my way. Soon, I was seeing a couple hundred patients a week, and my health started to suffer. When you work with energy, unless you know how to thoroughly clean it, you can take it on yourself. I was getting very tired, very pale, and having chest pains. It got to the point where it was a major struggle just to get out of my chair and walk to the door.

One morning, I was standing in front of a full-length mirror while getting dressed. When you look in a mirror, you can see your own aura. I happened to turn sideways and saw that my life cord, which is supposed to be attached deep into my heart chakra, had "unplugged" from the back of my heart and was hovering about twelve inches from where it should have been. I saw the life cord as a streaming trail of smoke, like what you see in a jet when it leaves a vapor trail. A clairvoyant healer can look at this stream, determine how fast the life cord is coming out, and estimate the person's time of death. From what I saw, I knew I had about six months left. I immediately saw a traditional medical doctor, who confirmed that I had advanced heart disease.

I tried to heal myself but nothing happened. I knew I needed to find somebody else. Since the heart is essentially about love, I thought, *Who can heal me and teach me to love?* Within days, somebody happened to mention that the Sufis were the true purveyors of love. Intrigued, I looked into Sufism and learned that the way of the Sufi is the way of love and quiet surrender to God. It is a lifestyle designed to weave the presence of divinity into even the most mundane aspects of our daily lives. I thought, *Yes, I need to find a Sufi teacher who can heal me.*

One of my students had heard that Sidi, a very high Sufi master who lived in Jerusalem, was coming to Santa Fe, which is about eight hours from Sedona. I drove out there to meet him. As far as I knew, he had no knowledge of my coming. And I had not told anybody about my heart condition. I don't even think my wife knew about it at that point.

As soon as I walked into his room, Sidi looked at me, closed his eyes for a moment, opened them, and said, "I have a message for you from Allah."

I said, "Allah, that's God, right?"

He replied, "Yes, Allah is the same as God."

I asked, "What is the message?"

He said, "Allah wants you to know that you have six months left to live." I was shocked, since that corresponded exactly with my estimate. He closed his eyes again and then said, "Allah has another message for you. You have six months left to live *if* you don't learn to love." His words rang true. Somehow my heart had closed, and I didn't know how to love in a deep way.

I asked, "Can you teach me?"

He said, "Yes, but you're going to have to 'take hand' with me and initiation with me. And you're going to have to forget everything you've learned and start fresh, so I can teach you how to be in the deep love. Are you willing to do that?"

I said, "Absolutely, I am." And in that moment, he initiated me. Instantly, I felt my heart open to the Sufi path of love, and I have been with him ever since. More than two decades after graduating medical school, traveling the world, and exploring various types of healing, I received my degree as a master spiritual healer from the Sufis.

My teaching today is essentially the same teaching as Sidi's, which is how to walk through the twenty-eight Sufi stations of the heart. These stations progressively take you deeper and deeper into experiencing more love, more connection, and more oneness with God until you eventually reach unity. And in that experience, a merging happens that we call God-realization. The light of God literally consumes your human nature, and your nature becomes one with divine nature. This was the process that Sidi walked me through for the first year of our relationship. Today, my heart is perfect; no problems whatsoever.

In my talks, I often mention the story about the doves. The teachings that the rabbis used to heal that girl came from the Talmud. I would say that today, when I work with people, I'm in that similar state. I'm receiving information directly from God and the angels about how to heal somebody using whatever methods God deems necessary for them. But more importantly, the core of my teaching is to show people how they can reach these states of divine knowledge and healing on their own.

All those years ago, when I had asked if I could hold one of the doves over the girl, the rabbis told me I needed to be a rabbi to be able to heal in that way. Now I see that the rabbis were saying, "You must be able to heal in the way of God." To do so, you must learn how to let go of all ego attachments, bow your heart in service to God first and then to the patient, and ask God to use you as His instrument for healing. Allah—God—alone is healer, and we are His vessels. This is the highest and most holy way of healing and being in the world that I have ever encountered.

32

DON JOSE LUIS

Don Jose Luis grew up in a world of magic, a gift of his heritage. His father, Toltec teacher Don Miguel Ruiz, author of The Four Agreements, *oversaw his training in the ancient Toltec wisdom of the native people of southern Mexico. This teaching was handed down to Don Miguel by his grandmother, Mother Sarita, a Toltec faith healer who learned the wisdom from her grandfather, Esiquio, a Toltec "nagual" or shaman. Through his workshops, steeped in Toltec wisdom, Don Jose shows participants how to illuminate their awareness and move toward transformation and authenticity. He also leads five-day Power Journeys to magnificent sacred sites in countries such as Mexico, Guatemala, and Peru. For more information, visit www.miguelruiz.com.*

In June 2001, I drove from Malibu to San Diego for a dentist appointment. On the way back, I started feeling a terrible pain in my eyes when I looked to either side. It even hurt to look in the rearview mirror. When I arrived home, I told my wife that my eyes hurt and that I was going to lie down. When I woke up, the pain was still in my eyes, and I couldn't see. I was very scared. I asked my wife to call my dad, who said to take me to see my aunt, an eye doctor in Tijuana, and that he would arrange for the family to meet me there. The pressure continued to build in my head as we drove to Tijuana.

After examining me, my aunt said I might never see again. I started to panic. I felt so desperate. I was admitted into a hospital, where I went into a deep meditation, beyond sound and sight. When my consciousness returned to the world around me, I was at peace. I sensed the fear and the pity of my family members, and I knew that, just as their suffering was a choice, I could choose to be either the ultimate victim who was stuck in a bad dream or a great warrior who accepts the gift of life and everything it brings. That realization allowed me to surrender to love and let go of fear. My family was so worried, but I knew I would be okay. I was the blind one, but I ended up consoling them. I knew that even if I were blind, nothing could take my heaven away. I only had to have faith in myself and in God.

I had always loved to look in people's eyes. I could see in their eyes a reflection of the love I felt for them. It was a powerful connection. But I started to detach from my eyesight, knowing I could still connect with others through my hands, my emotions, and my inner perceptions.

A week and a half after losing my sight, I dreamed I was walking in a desert and came upon a cave. In that cave were many light bodies. With love, I directed the bodies to fly into the sun. I entered the cave and saw many demons. I was not afraid because I knew if something happened to me, I would be going back to the sun to be with my Creator. I elevated myself and said, "Take me to your leader." I floated up and was with a large demon, Saint Lucifer himself.

He looked into my eyes and said, "How dare you take my souls away and send them into the sun!"

And I said, "You've forgotten, haven't you? They belong to the sun, and I belong to the sun, as you belong to the sun." He laughed in mockery and then jumped and bit my neck. I was not afraid. I surrendered. And I looked back, forgiving each moment of my life. I could see my own self looking at me in total forgiveness. After that dream, I was in total surrender. I knew I could be banished and still love, surrender, and forgive in each moment. Life is just a dream, and in forgiving and loving others, we are loving the Creator.

Three days after that dream, I was given my eyesight back. I woke up that morning and could see light coming in my room. It was so beautiful—the emotion of seeing my hands, of seeing my wife's eyes, of seeing all the love and gratitude I had for the world. Life is short, and each moment is ours to love and forgive, to live life, to not let ourselves be imprisoned by our thoughts and fears. Everyone believes in lies, and that makes the fear grow. The lie is that God is not inside each of us, that we are separate from God. We must let God be free in us. That is total freedom. It is true enlightenment—to live your dream, to live your life, to just be happy. It is so beautiful, this celebration of life. It is the dream of God.

33

DEAN ORNISH, M.D.

Dr. Ornish is the founder, president, and director of the nonprofit Preventive Medicine Research Institute in Sausalito, California. For the past thirty years, he has directed clinical research demonstrating, for the first time, that comprehensive lifestyle changes may begin to reverse the progression of even severe coronary heart disease and prostate cancer without drugs or surgery. He is the author of five best-selling books, including New York Times *bestsellers* Dr. Dean Ornish's Program for Reversing Heart Disease; Eat More, Weigh Less; *and* Love and Survival. *Dr. Ornish was recognized as "one of the most interesting people of 1996" by* People *magazine, featured in the "Time 100" issue on alternative medicine, and chosen by* Life *magazine as "one of the 50 most influential members of his generation." For more information, visit www.ornish.com and www.pmri.org.*

After finishing high school in Dallas, I began studying at Rice University, a small, extremely competitive university in Houston. Over half the students there had graduated either first or second from their high school, and most of them acted as though academic success would define their net worth. It did for me. It's no surprise that Rice also had the highest suicide rate per capita of any school in the country.

From the beginning, I worried that I wouldn't do well enough to be accepted to medical school. I got into a vicious cycle—the more I worried, the harder it became to study; the harder it was to study, the more I worried. My mind was racing so fast that I couldn't sleep. I would lie down and watch the hands of the clock go around and around until morning. At one point, this went on for about ten days in a row.

Becoming that sleep-deprived is enough to make anyone a little crazy, and I got to the point where I couldn't function at all. I became deeply depressed for two reasons: one, I thought I was stupid and a fraud, that I had somehow managed to fool people into thinking that I was smart, and now that I was in a school with a lot of really smart people, it was just a matter of time before they figured out what a mistake they had made by letting me in; and two, which was even more painful, I had a spiritual vision before I was ready to handle it. And that vision was *Nothing can bring lasting happiness*. The combination of those—feeling like I was never going to amount to anything, and even if I did, it wouldn't matter—was profoundly depressing.

The worst thing about being depressed, as opposed to just being sad or blue, is that you really feel like you're seeing the world clearly for the first time, that all the other times you ever thought you'd be happy, you were just deluding yourself. And that's where that hopelessness and helplessness come from, because it's not that you just feel bad today, you feel like you're always going to feel bad and there's nothing anyone can do about it. That's true depression, and it's a lot more common in our culture than most people realize.

I remember one day very clearly—I was sitting in my organic chemistry class when it occurred to me, *I'm in so much emotional pain. I'm so tired. I'll just kill myself and be done with it. Then I can sleep and be at peace forever*. It seemed so logical and clear; I couldn't imagine why I hadn't thought of it before. And in the twisted logic of the moment, some part of me replied, "Because you're stupid, that's why!"

I had always thought that if I could get into medical school, become a doctor, make a lot of money, get married and have kids, then I'd be happy. I now realized that those things weren't going to bring me happiness. I remember being in my apartment and looking around at all the material possessions that were supposed to make me happy, and the idea seemed like a cruel joke. I threw my expensive stereo down a flight of stairs.

I was very depressed and getting increasingly worse. I was so run down that I got a really bad case of mononucleosis. I was so ill that I didn't have the energy to get out of bed. It was my first understanding of how the mind can affect the body, in this case for the worse. When my parents saw how sick I was, they told me to withdraw from school and come back to Dallas, which I did. I felt like a complete failure. I was very anxious to get well enough to go out and kill myself.

Then something happened that changed everything. My older sister, Laurel, had been studying yoga and meditation with the renowned ecumenical spiritual teacher, Swami Satchidananda. She had become happier and calmer and had stopped getting migraine headaches. As a gesture of support for her, my parents hosted a cocktail party for the swami. This was considered a little strange back in 1972, especially in Texas.

He walked in our front door looking like a casting agent's idea of a swami—he had a long white beard; intelligent, sparkling, and peaceful eyes; and he was wearing long saffron robes. There's an old saying, "When the student is ready, the teacher appears," and that was certainly true for me. He had agreed to conduct a satsang, or informal lecture, in our living room. He started off by saying, "Nothing can bring you lasting happiness," which I'd already figured out—except he was glowing and radiantly happy, and I was miserable and ready to kill myself.

The second half of his sentence sounded like a New Age cliché, and yet it turned my life around: "Nothing can bring you lasting happiness, but you have it already until you disturb it." He went on to say, "Not being mindful of that, we end up running after all the things that we think are going to make us happy. And in the process, we disturb the peace, happiness, and well-being that we already have if we simply quiet down the mind and body enough to experience it."

It's a radical concept, and it goes against everything we learn in our culture. The entire advertising industry is based on the idea that if we just get these things outside of ourselves we think we're lacking, they'll bring us happiness. And they do for a very short period of time, which is what makes them so seductive. But it's soon followed by, "Now what?" because it's never enough, or "So what?" because it doesn't provide a lasting sense of meaning, joy, and peace. In some ways, it's even more painful to get all the things you think are going to make you happy and then realize they don't than it is to not have them—at least then you still believe in the myth that happiness would be yours if only you could get them. That's why some of the most unhappy people are often the most affluent and powerful—they can't tell themselves that if they just had a little more money, or a little more power, or a little more influence, they'd be happy.

Anyway, I was in so much emotional pain that I was willing to try anything. It's not even so much *what* the swami said but *who he was* and what he embodied. I was struck by the clear light that was filling up the room, his peacefulness and playfulness, the twinkle in his eye, and the joy that he exuded. And so I figured, *Well, let me give this a try. I can always go to Plan B and kill myself if it doesn't work.* So I gave up my Texas diet of chili, chalupas, and cheeseburgers; began exercising, meditating, doing yoga, practicing breathing and relaxation techniques; and started doing more selfless service. Within days, I began to get glimpses of what he was talking about, and that was enough to save me.

A few weeks later, I went back to school with a lighter course load and then went on to summer school to make up the rest of the courses I had missed. After that, I transferred to the University of Texas at Austin and did so well that I actually graduated first in my class and gave the commencement address. I went from one end of the spectrum to the other because of the difference in my intention. And that was part of the paradox: The degree to which I felt like I had to do well in school—*so* I could get into medical school *so* I could become a doctor *so* I could be happy—had stressed me out so much that I couldn't sleep. I couldn't function. I couldn't read a headline in a newspaper and tell you ten minutes later what it said. But to the degree that I was more inwardly defined, the less I needed to succeed and the less stressed I felt, which allowed me to function at a much higher level. Paradoxically then, the less I needed success, the easier it came to me.

Once I made the connection between when I felt stressed and why, then stress became my teacher instead of my enemy. When I felt angry, afraid, anxious, or depressed, the suffering and stress reminded me that I was looking in the wrong places for peace and happiness and self-esteem. I stopped viewing pain—both physical and emotional—as punishment and began seeing it as information. It was an empowering realization. If I felt I didn't have any control over a situation, if I was just a victim of bad luck, bad karma, bad genes, bad fate, or whatever, then what could I do? I was helpless. But if the answer lay within me, then I could do something about it. That's why, when people asked the swami, "What are you, a Hindu?" he'd say, "No, I'm an Undo. I'm trying to teach people how they can undo the patterns that cause damage to their minds and bodies so they can begin to heal." It's all about having the awareness to identify and to stop doing the things that allow our inner peace to be disturbed.

I talked to the swami almost once a week for more than thirty years. We traveled all over the world together and had a very close personal relationship until the day he died. I still practice his teachings today—it's called a "practice" because you never master it, you just keep going deeper—which form the basis of the lifestyle program my colleagues and I created to help people stop, and even reverse, the progression of heart disease and other chronic diseases.

Many people focus on the nutrition aspect of our program, but diet is really the least interesting aspect of it. It's really about transformation. And in particular, it's about helping people use the experience of suffering as a doorway for transforming their lives. Depression was my doorway; for someone else, it might be a heart attack, or a divorce, or a child who gets sick, or any of a number of painful, traumatic things that people experience. And while I would never go up to someone who is suffering and say, "Oh, how wonderful, you have this opportunity to transform"—the proper response to that would be a punch in the nose—suffering is a part of life. All too often, there it is. If we can use our suffering as a catalyst for fundamentally transforming our lives, then it brings meaning to the suffering and makes it more bearable.

After doing research on people with heart disease, I also realized that their physical problems were just the tip of the iceberg; in many cases, they were suffering from many of the same issues I had struggled with—depression, loneliness, isolation, and lack of meaning in their lives. When we began working on that level and addressing the psychic, social, emotional, and spiritual dimensions of heart disease, then their physical heart disease also improved in ways that we could actually measure. Ironically, we used very high-tech, expensive, state-of-the-art measures to prove the power of these low-tech, low-cost, and in many ways, ancient interventions.

If you don't try to address suffering at a deeper level, it's very difficult to motivate people to make and maintain any kind of meaningful changes in their diet and lifestyle, or even to take their medications. If you had told me back when I was so depressed that I was going to live longer if I just did this or that, I would've said, "You don't understand. I don't know if I want to live longer. I don't know if I want to live at all." And so part of what we learned is that providing people with health information is important but not usually sufficient to motivate them to make lasting changes in their behavior. If it were, nobody would smoke because everybody knows it's not good for you. People smoke or overeat or use alcohol or drugs to numb their pain. Or they work too hard or spend too much time on the Internet or watching TV to distract themselves from their pain. I used to ask my patients why they engaged in such maladaptive behaviors until I kept hearing the reply, "You know, Dean, you don't have a clue. These behaviors aren't maladaptive. They're very adaptive because they help me get through the day."

The problem is, we just kill the pain or numb it or bypass it without listening to it; it's a little like clipping the wires to a fire alarm and going back to sleep while your house keeps burning. It just gets worse because you haven't dealt with it. And so much of what we do in traditional Western medicine is like clipping the wires to a fire alarm rather than addressing the under-lying cause.

Change is hard. But if you're in enough pain, as I was when I was in college, suddenly the idea of change becomes more inter-esting. And when people make the kinds of changes in their lives that I recommend, most of them find that they feel so much bet-ter so quickly, it reframes the reason for making those changes from simply living longer to living better, from fear of dying to joy of living. And because of that, many of them will look back on painful events and think, as I did, *I wouldn't wish what I went through on anyone, but I never would have been motivated to even explore the areas that have made such a profound difference in my life had I not gone through that pain at the time.*

I know I wouldn't be here today were it not for Swami Satchidananda and his teachings. Just as others passed these teachings on to him, passing on this wisdom to others is my dharma now. This wisdom is part of all spiritual traditions and religions once we get past the superficial differences. The more I experience the inner peace and love that are already fully present in everyone, the wider I am able to open my heart to my wife and true love, Anne, and son, Lucas, in ways that have made my life more joyful than anything I could have ever imagined.

34

JAMES REDFIELD

Redfield's first book, The Celestine Prophecy, *an adventure parable about a spiritual journey to Peru, was a global phenomenon. In 1995 and 1996, it was the top-selling American book in the world. The sequel,* The Tenth Insight: Holding the Vision, *was published in 1996. The two books combined to make Redfield the bestselling hardcover author in the world that year. The third book in the series,* The Secret of Shambhala: In Search of the Eleventh Insight, *was published in 1999. Redfield also cowrote the screenplay for the film version of* The Celestine Prophecy, *which premiered in April 2006. For more information, visit www.celestinevision.com.*

Back in 1973, I was hiking in Great Smoky Mountains National Park on the North Carolina side. I must have been two miles deep in the woods, far away from any roads, just getting in touch with the beauty of the pristine, old-growth forest. Suddenly, I had what I call a birth vision, which is a remembrance of the intentions I had for this lifetime before incarnating on the planet.

The first thing I noticed was that everything became incredibly beautiful. Colors were deeper, lights were brighter, and the world seemed to turn more spiritual. Trees were no longer just trees but living entities. I felt lifted into a higher self-wisdom and deeply connected to the environment around me.

The vision began by showing me how I had begun walking my spiritual path. I saw myself at fourteen or fifteen, beginning to explore the spiritual dimensions of life. I was reading Norman

Vincent Peale and Ruth Montgomery, wondering about everything from the effects of positive thinking to angelic contact to communicating with departed loved ones. Then, in college, I studied different religions and philosophies while majoring in sociology. As I relived these experiences, I realized they had been preparing me for what was to come.

Then the vision went into the future. It showed me highlights of everything that was going to happen to me creatively—everything that I was going to create and offer to the world over the next few decades. I saw myself developing my spiritual philosophy and writing books that would help awaken people all over the world to a deeper spirituality. I saw that I would be making at least one movie and presenting lectures on cultural evolution and spiritual development. Although it was essentially a vision of my possible future, it felt more like a memory of what I wanted to accomplish in this life.

The vision lasted quite a while in spiritual time because I lived out very specific events and experiences. It wasn't focused only on what I was supposed to deliver into the world; it also showed me the growth steps I needed to take in order to accomplish it all. In real time, however, it probably lasted only four or five minutes.

And then it was gone and I was back in the forest. It was a transcendent experience, terribly exciting and inspiring and energizing. That feeling stayed with me about a week before it started to fade. Being only twenty-one and never having written anything, I started to doubt whether what I saw was true, whether it was something I could or would become. I wondered if it was all just a pipe dream. I spent the next fifteen years as a counselor working with emotionally disturbed and abused adolescents.

Over the years, however, I consciously worked at improving the way I expressed myself, both in my writing and in my public speaking. Even back in school, I had felt intuitively that I should be improving my skills in those areas, although like most people, I had some hesitancy about my qualifications. I thought, *Who am I to be writing and giving speeches about my ideas?* I had to develop more self-confidence and get past that natural reluctance we all have about sticking out. I also made a point to bring up spiritual topics and go deeper in my personal conversations. I wasn't sure what all this was leading to, but the memory of my vision had lingered, and it had been very clearly presented to me that I would need to do these things if I was going to accomplish anything I had seen.

Then, in my mid-thirties, the things I saw in my vision began to actually occur. And as I developed and refined the spiritual psychology that would eventually form the basis of *The Celestine Prophecy*, the memory of that birth vision was triggered. I remembered that the vision had very clearly showed me that I would be writing and speaking about twelve insights, although I hadn't understood what that meant at the time. So when I wrote *The Celestine Prophecy*, although nine insights felt just right for that book, I knew there would be twelve in all. However, I only had a vague sense of what the last three would be.

As I observed the culture and my own experiences, the tenth insight started to come in, and I knew that that would be the next book. Three years after I finished *The Celestine Prophecy*, I completed *The Tenth Insight*. And three years after that, I finished The *Secret of Shambhala: In Search of the Eleventh Insight*. The twelfth insight seems to be coming together now, so I'll be writing one more book. After that, I'll be devoting most of my time to social commentary.

I'm now fifty-three, and the end of this decade is where my memory of what I saw in my vision starts to fade in its clarity. So I'm sure that will be the beginning of a whole new adventure.

35

MALIDOMA PATRICE SOMÉ

Malidoma, an initiated elder in his village of Dano in Burkina Faso, West Africa, is also a medicine man and diviner in the Dagara culture. As a representative of his culture, he has come to the West to share the ancient wisdom and practices that have supported his people for thousands of years. He has authored Of Water and the Spirit: Ritual, Magic, and Initiation in the Life of an African Shaman; Ritual: Power, Healing, and Community; *and* Healing Wisdom of Africa. *For more information, visit www.malidoma.com.*

When the elders in my village approached me about becoming initiated into elderhood, my reaction was, *Why me, of all people?* There were others in the village who were great healers with fantastic track records, and I was nowhere near their level. I had always been fascinated with the traditions of my culture, but at forty-three, I considered myself too young to be an elder. Besides, I lived in the white man's culture and only came home once in a while.

They told me that, yes, I lived in the white man's country, but that every time I came home with a dozen white people from America or England or Europe, as I often did, they saw that I was playing the role of a bridge. It was through that function that it had become possible for them to realize that the white man does not hate our tradition, does not despise our ritual—that, in fact, the white man would like to find in our medicine something that will help him heal, something that can bring his culture closer to ours.

Therefore, they could see in my bridge-building role something that would match the function of an elder. I was living in two worlds and helping those worlds come together into a circle of understanding, a circle that was bringing our traditions the kind of respect that they had thought modern culture could never give.

That was why, every time I brought people with me to the village, they would take time out from their regular schedule to devote their attention to these visitors. They explained that these white people were only here for a limited time, and therefore needed to return with the right impression, needed to return with the right attitude.

Their reasons were convincing, and I agreed to be initiated. Although I would also be responsible for the maintenance of three shrines, the primary responsibility of the council of elders was to ensure the continuity of the community through initiation. This requires the five elders to sit together to consider various candidacies. The candidates don't have to apply; they are picked and then informed about it.

It was at the end of my initiation that I realized I had reached a point of no return. I had become privy to ancient knowledge, and it felt like this information was welded into my body. There are a lot of supernatural things going on during an initiation, things so mind-boggling that seeing how they were done changed me completely.

It's one thing to be the subject upon whom these magical things happen. It's another thing to be in the shoes of the one instigating them and knowing how to wield the various ingredients in order to open the vortexes, the doorways, leading to other worlds.

After my initiation, my psyche changed so dramatically that my mind could not operate the way it used to operate any longer. For a while, I was very, very serious, with the "little human me" questioning my deservedness and then questioning my ability to hold on to this precious information. These two concerns were pressing upon me so hard that I felt very dense and weighed down. So I looked very serious, and probably flabbergasted, like someone who had been permanently stunned.

And so my initiation as an elder was first experienced as a burden. For a couple years, I longed to return to that state where I was in a place of free leadership, the kind of leadership that doesn't come with intense accountability. I had been making it up as I went along, defining myself as a free-flow choreographer who was simply doing his best to explain the spiritual values and traditions of my people.

My initiation had taken my identification with my people to a whole different level. I was no longer just another person who happened to be living in the Western world and was respectful of the tradition. I was now the one officially installed to be the protector, the keeper, the one to maintain the integrity of these values. I was no longer just the spokesman in the West, but also in the tribe and in Africa in general. I, therefore, fully became a man of two worlds. I realized that I would be going home not so much to try to make sure that simple rituals were followed, but to join with my peers in an attempt to revisit the main tenets of the culture that the council of elders was in charge of, was responsible for maintaining and servicing.

The changes in my life were not just mental but also behavioral. I could no longer feel free to hang out wherever I wished. I could no longer be seen in certain places that I considered "low places." I could no longer just walk into parties like a person who needed some fun time. As I mentioned, I noticed myself becoming dangerously serious—serious in the sense that I felt myself limited, as if I had become imprisoned in a straitjacket that I wanted to break out of.

I haven't yet resolved this, but I've been learning more about how to be with myself, about how to be secluded and feel good about it. That's part of the reason why I moved to Eugene, Oregon. I needed to live in a nature setting, so my social time is largely spent amongst nature and trees.

I've also become more accustomed to not going to parties. In fact, I've noticed a certain amount of discomfort rising from within me every time I'm socializing because something about me has become estranged. I don't know how to enjoy that anymore. There have been times when I've been dragged to parties and felt completely out of place. The only thing I was thinking was, *Go home, you have no business here*. I can't tell where that comes from. Maybe it is because I've spent so much time all by myself that I've forgotten the fun naturally associated with parties, or maybe something did take hold inside of me that deleted the pleasure naturally available at social events.

However, the most frustrating thing to come from my initiation was that there were rules and regulations that were impossible to separate from. One thing people need to understand about African medicine is that it is intimately connected to the science of nature. As such, it is following an epistemology that is not available to the scientific inquiry currently upheld in modernity. There are tremendous scientific breakthroughs held together by nature. This is why indigenous people love to keep nature the way it is, because any disruption of nature is likely to disrupt the structure of the information in it.

During elders initiation, a sequence of "passwords" is disclosed, thanks to which it becomes possible to hear the voice of nature, thereby leading to the intimate knowledge of what it takes to accomplish the kind of thing that Westerners view as super-natural or magical.

At first, I was dying to share, to present, to explore this knowledge. I felt it was my duty as an elder and a bridge-builder to be able to change the standing of my culture by allowing the hidden part of its wisdom to become seeable, touchable, in a way that would enable this consciousness to reach the modern world as dramatically as possible—so the respect that the indigenous elders are getting now can reach the sky, so big that it will feel like those indigenous elders are right here in the West as they are there, just the same way that the West is present everywhere.

I felt strongly that if I was to be a bridge, I shouldn't just be focused on bringing ritual and healing work to the West but also I should try to find a way of making this wisdom available to the world because it has the power to transform human conscious-ness. I now saw the truth in the idea that the redemption of the world resides in the hands of the indigenous.

Yet this oath of secrecy I have taken is perhaps another one of my burdens, because this ancient wisdom comes with a sort of built-in self-destruct should the information be improperly dis-closed. Think of it as a burglar alarm that would be set off the minute that something is said or done that leads to an exposure of that which can only stay alive if it remains hidden. If exposed, it starts to lose its life; and as it starts to lose its life, the carrier of that information who broke the rule is also in a state of grave dan-ger, not only of being exposed to emotional trauma but to physi-cal trauma as well.

Recently, I had some medicine put into my body as a safety net. Now, if I speak too close to the secret, I will start hearing loud noises in my ears, which remind me that I'm getting too close. So the dilemma that I'm facing is that, speaking from a Western perspective, this information deriving from the science of nature could change the material life of the entire tribe, bringing it to par with the Western lifestyle. In other words, there is in it enough to bring tremendous abundance to the people who are the keeper of it.

And I now have knowledge of various powerful ways of exploding Western consciousness into parallel dimensions, to jack up modern consciousness to the next level. This wisdom could perhaps make modernity much more aware of the human intimacy with nature and how that intimacy can translate into something very nourishing to mind, body, and spirit, and redemptive to the issue of community, of family, and the sense of the innate gift that people are said to come into the world with. In sharing these gifts, the world could then swim in endless abundance.

I personally hold a deep hope that this is going to happen. I don't want to become a renegade elder. I don't want to become an elder who's estranged. I want to be the elder who allows the minds of my co-elders to expand sufficiently so that they can, in the end, see the world the way I see it. And by seeing it that way, they can then understand why it is so important that their wisdom become a major contributor to world consciousness.

36

BILLY VERA

Singer/songwriter Vera made his first record and wrote a chart hit for Ricky Nelson while still in his teens. In 1985, four years after his band, Billy Vera and the Beaters, had recorded "At This Moment," the song was used in the hit sitcom Family Ties, *which rocketed both the song and Vera to stardom. Also an accomplished actor, Vera has appeared in numerous movies and television shows and is a sought-after voice-over artist. Billy Vera and the Beaters has established itself as the quintessential L.A. band; Hollywood stars and other celebrities frequently attend their shows throughout the Southern California area. For more information, visit www.billyvera.com and myspace.com/billyvera.*

I n January 1979, I had just signed a three-year songwriting and publishing deal with Warner Bros. Music Publishing. I was living in New York, so I threw everything I owned in my car and drove out to L.A. Ed Silvers, the head of Warner Bros., wanted his staff to hear my songs to get them excited about working the material, so I put on a concert in Ed's office. After singing "At This Moment," I turned around and here was this cynical, hardened record-business guy crying in front of his staff. So I knew I had something.

Not long after moving to L.A., I ran into Chuck Fiore, my former bass player in New York. We decided to start a band just to have some fun and meet some girls. That's how Billy Vera and the Beaters was born. In 1981, we signed a record deal with Alfa

Records, a Japanese-owned company, and had a mid-chart hit that year with "I Can Take Care of Myself." The second single we released was "At This Moment," but the timing was terrible. Alfa went out of business, and the song reached only the bottom of the charts. We were without a record deal for the next five years, during which I supported myself through acting and playing clubs.

And then one day, I got a phone call from a guy who said that he had seen the band the previous weekend and that he produced *Family Ties*, the number-two television show in the country. He said he wanted to use "At This Moment" on the show. I wasn't that excited because, from time to time, songs of mine were used on different shows. To me, it just meant a few hundred bucks.

I put him in touch with Warner Bros., which administered licensing rights for my songs. After the show aired in September 1985, I got a bag full of mail from NBC, which told me that, *Hey, people like this song. Maybe I should see if I can interest a record company in letting me re-record it.* But everywhere I went, the answer was no.

Finally, one day I was having lunch with Richard Foos, the owner of Rhino Records, a label that specializes in reissues of older music. I told him the story, and he expressed interest. I asked him, "How many records do you need to sell to break even on an album release?" He said about two thousand—they obviously had low overhead. I said, "If I can guarantee you two thousand sales, and if my lawyer can facilitate a deal between you and the Japanese company that owns the master recordings, would you put out an album containing 'At This Moment'?"

He said, "Sure, why not?" By the time we got the record out, however, we had missed the reruns of *Family Ties*, so nothing much came of it.

The next year, I was hired to write three songs in a movie called *Blind Date*, which starred Bruce Willis and Kim Basinger.

I was living in a garden apartment and would often see an old lady who lived in an apartment building across the courtyard from me. Behind my building was a delicatessen; I'd see the old lady there, and we had a nodding acquaintance. At the time, my mother, who was dying of cancer, decided to give me an advance on my inheritance so I could buy a house; she wanted to see her son have a house rather than pay rent the rest of his life.

A couple days before I moved out of the apartment, I ran into the old lady in the deli. I said, "Well, we won't be meeting like this anymore. I'm moving."

She said, "Oh, yes, you'll be very happy in your new home." I looked at her kind of funny, because that was an odd thing to say. She said, "You don't know me, but I'm a psychic." I just smiled politely because I wasn't a believer in that stuff. She asked, "You're in show business, right?" I said to myself, Y*eah, well, that's an easy guess. Everybody in Hollywood is in show business or wants to be.* And she said, "You write songs." And then she said, "I see a song that you wrote being big beyond your wildest dreams."

I said, "Well, I have three songs coming out in a movie in the next few months."

She said, "No, I see this on television." I just looked at her, and she said, "In fact, it's a song that you wrote nine years ago. You didn't finish it right away. It took you another year to finish this song."

Well, the only song it could have possibly been was "At This Moment." I almost always complete a song in one day, but in the case of that song, that's exactly how it happened. I had started it nine years before but wasn't able to finish it. A girl I had just started dating had very vividly told me how her previous boyfriend had reacted when she broke up with him. So I went home and wrote the first two-thirds of the song from what I perceived as his point of view. But I couldn't figure out how to end it. A year later, when she dumped me, that's when I knew how it ended.

After leaving the deli, I didn't think any more about what the old lady had said. But to my surprise, just two weeks later, in October 1986, *Family Ties* used "At This Moment" again, in the second episode of the new season. And this time, the story of the song, *boy loses girl*, matched the story of the episode, in which the girl breaks up with Michael J. Fox's character. This time, the audience went crazy. NBC said they got more letters and phone calls than any other time in the history of the network for a song. And this time, we had a record out on the market.

And that rare thing happened—there was a grassroots demand. That was a good thing because Rhino, not being in the business of promoting or even releasing current records, had no idea how to promote a song on the radio. So without payola or any promotion to speak of, the song barreled up the charts to number one, where it stayed for two weeks and became one of the biggest selling records of the year.

I was forty-two years old when this happened. I had had a couple of hits in the '60s, nothing in the '70s, and here I was in 1987, and I've got the number-one record in the country at an age when you're not even a contender in the record business; rock 'n' roll is a young man's game. Nevertheless, it completely changed my life. Suddenly, I was on *The Tonight Show* nine times. I was on every show that plays popular music. My dream of appearing on *American Bandstand* finally came true. Even my acting career picked up, and I started appearing in more movies and television shows.

Since I was that rarity, a free agent with a number-one record, I was besieged by presidents of major record companies. People I couldn't get on the phone a month earlier were begging me to sign with them. I chose Capitol Records, but the subsequent album failed to ignite. Who knows why. It may not have been commercial enough, or I may have been too old to appeal to fourteen-year-old kids.

Even so, I was now in "the club." I was now somebody who had a name. People would come to me for other kinds of work. I began to produce albums for other artists like Lou Rawls. I got into a voice-over career, which continues to this day. And because of my knowledge of older music, I began to compile and anthologize reissues of older music for Rhino and other record companies.

So as a result of that one record, I've been able to make a good living for myself ever since. I often think, *Had that not happened, what would have happened to me?* I'm sixty-three now, and I've seen what happens to musicians when they reach that age without having had a hit record or any other meaningful success. They scuffle and struggle the rest of their days. So I was extremely lucky, thanks to that one song.

Moments of Enlightenment

37

GREGG BRADEN

Braden, a bestselling author and internationally renowned speaker, is a pioneer in bridging the wisdom of our past with the science, healing, and peace of our future. After serving as a senior computer systems designer for Martin Marietta Aerospace, a computer geologist for Phillips Petroleum, and the technical operations manager for Cisco Systems, Braden's work is now devoted to inspiring humanity to build a better world. His books include The Divine Matrix, The God Code, *and* The Isaiah Effect. *For more information, visit www.greggbraden.com.*

Back in the early '90s, I was living in the high desert of northern New Mexico. This was during one of the worst droughts that the Southwest had ever recorded. The elders in the native pueblos said that, as far back as they could remember, they'd never gone so long without rain.

David, a native friend of mine from one of those nearby pueblos, called me one summer morning and asked if I wanted to join him in visiting a place his ancestors had built where he would pray for rain. I agreed, and soon we were hiking through hundreds of acres of high desert sage. He led me to a place where there was a stone circle that reminded me of a medicine wheel. Each stone had been placed precisely by the hands of his ancestors long ago.

I had an expectation of what I thought I was going to see. But my friend simply removed his hiking boots and then stepped with his naked feet into the stone circle. The first thing he did was honor all of his ancestors. Then he held his hands in a prayer position in front of his chest, turned his back to me, and closed his eyes. Less than a minute later, he turned around and said, "I'm hungry. Let's go get a bite to eat."

Surprised, I said, "I thought you came here to pray for rain." I had been expecting to see some chanting and dancing.

He looked at me and said, "No. If I prayed *for* rain, the rain could never happen." When I asked him why, he said it's because the moment you pray for something to occur, you've just acknowledged that it's not existing in that moment—and you may actually be denying the very thing you'd like to bring forward in your prayers.

"Well, if you didn't pray for rain just now when you closed your eyes," I said, "what *did* you do?"

He said, "When I closed my eyes, I felt the feeling of what it feels like after there's been so much rain that I can stand with my naked feet in the mud of my pueblo village. I smelled the smells of rainwater rolling off the earthen walls of our homes. And I felt what it feels like to walk through a field of corn that is chest high because of all the rain that has fallen. In that way, I plant a seed for the possibility of that rain, and then I give thanks of gratitude and appreciation."

I said, "You mean gratitude for the rain that you've created?"

And he said, "No, we don't create the rain. I'm giving thanks of gratitude and appreciation for the opportunity to commune with the forces of creation."

That explanation really resonated with me because I've since learned that the word *prayer* doesn't show up in any ancient traditions. You don't see it in the Dead Sea Scrolls; you don't see it on ancient temple walls. *Prayer* is a relatively recent word. The word we do find is the word *commune* or *communion*.

That makes perfect sense because quantum science now acknowledges that a field of intelligent energy connects all of creation and that all of us are in communion with that field in every moment through the language of feeling. Feeling is the union of thought and emotion. When we embody a feeling, the outer world mirrors for us what our inner world has created. Whether we choose love, joy, fear, or anger, the world mirrors back to us those same qualities because the world honors the principles of creation.

David didn't tell me any of that, of course. From his perspective of the ancient ways, he simply said that if we feel as if the prayer has already happened, we give it the energy to come forth in our lives. And that implies that when we pray *for* something to happen, we may be actually contributing to the very conditions we would like to change.

It was early afternoon, so we went to get a bite to eat. By the time we got back, big black clouds were hanging over the Sangre de Cristo mountains. That night, it began to rain for the first time in months. It rained all through the night, into the next morning, and throughout the afternoon. In the early evening, I called David and said, "Wow, this is a mess. It hasn't stopped raining since last night. The fields are flooding and the roads are washed out between here and the nearest town. What's going on?"

He was silent for a moment, and then he chuckled and said, "That's the part of the prayer that my ancestors could never figure out."

Fast-forward to 1998. I was leading a twenty-two-day pilgrimage into the highlands of central China and into Tibet. During that period, I had the opportunity to visit twelve monasteries and two nunneries. My day in the desert with David had left quite an impression on me, so I asked every monk and nun a question that linked back to that day and to David's prayer.

In the traditions of the Tibetans, there has always been a modality of prayer that has no words, no outward expression, and doesn't fit into the models of prayer that we use here in the West. So I asked an abbot, "We see you praying twelve hours a day; we smell the incense; we hear the chants, the mantras, the mudras, the bells, the gongs. We see the healings and the effects of your prayers on the outside. But what are you doing on the inside?"

The abbot looked at me and said, "Well, you've never *seen* our prayers because a prayer is something that can't be seen. What you've seen are the things we do to create the feelings in our bodies and the feelings of prayers."

Based on what we now know of the quantum field, the abbot's words made perfect sense to me. In a single sentence, he had described this mode of prayer precisely the way David had shared with me his traditions nearly ten years earlier. What both of them were saying is that feeling *is* the prayer and that we all have the ability to commune directly with the forces of nature around us. This means that rather than feeling like helpless observers, we have the opportunity to participate in events as they unfold.

It was the combination of these two events that confirmed my belief in our role as co-creators in this world. And just as quantum physicists are now saying that it is our "observation" of the world around us that changes that world, the abbot was describing how to "observe" the external world from within in a way that can indeed bring changes.

This means, as scientists like John Wheeler of Princeton University are now telling us, that we can no longer see ourselves as passive observers casually strolling through the universe, that the act of being conscious in creation is an act of creation unto itself. And while I understood this intellectually, I never truly felt what it meant—until I tied together my conversation with a Tibetan abbot and a summer afternoon spent with my Native American friend.

38

DEEPAK CHOPRA, M.D.

Dr. Chopra, a pioneer of alternative medicine, has melded modern theories of quantum physics with the timeless wisdom of ancient cultures to change the way the world views physical, mental, emotional, spiritual, and social wellness. His Chopra Centers in New York City and Carlsbad, California, focus on enhancing health and nourishing the human spirit. Dr. Chopra's more than forty-nine books and more than one hundred audio, video, and CD-ROM titles have been translated into thirty-five languages and have sold over twenty million copies worldwide. His books include Peace Is the Way; The Book of Secrets: Unlocking the Hidden Dimensions of your Life; The Seven Spiritual Laws of Success; The Spontaneous Fulfillment of Desire: Harnessing the Infinite Power of Coincidence; *and* Ageless Body, Timeless Mind. *For more information, visit www.deepakchopra.com.*

My grandfather and I were very close. When I was six years old, my father was training in cardiology in England. One day my grandfather took us to the movies and the circus and then out for dinner. That night, he died in his sleep. The next day, it was as if he had disappeared. I remember even at six years of age saying to myself, *One day I'm going to find out what happens after we die.*

In January 2001, my father passed away, and I had to go to India to cremate his body. Part of the ritual was to bathe his body and anoint it with oil. I then carried his body over my shoulder, put it on a funeral pyre, and lit the fire to make sure his body was totally cremated. Part of the ritual was also to crack the skull with a stick to make sure that everything ultimately disappears. The next day, you are to come and collect the ashes, which are little pieces of bone about the size of a quarter, and throw them into the flowing Ganges. It takes about forty-eight hours to do all this.

I never felt closer to my father than I did during this whole experience. I could feel his presence and his spirit and his love and the intimacy that I had with him. I experienced my entire life unrolling before my eyes on the screen of my consciousness— every conversation we'd had, every game we'd played since childhood. And I recalled things he had told me about his childhood and his parents and so forth. It was the clearest experience I've had of timelessness, of love, and of connectedness with the universe.

While I was cremating him, about two hundred yards away, there was a group of children who were using the draft of the cremation fire to fly their kite. I could see in this the play of life and death. The kite was like the symbol of the spirit soaring into the heavens.

39

DAN MILLMAN

Millman, a former world-champion gymnast, martial arts instructor, and college professor, has for three decades explored the heart of the spiritual traditions. His keynotes, seminars, and trainings present practical ways to live with a peaceful heart and warrior spirit. Millman's twelve books have inspired millions of readers in twenty-nine languages, and his work has influenced people from all walks of life. His first book, Way of the Peaceful Warrior, *was made into a motion picture starring Nick Nolte. For more information, visit www.peacefulwarrior.com.*

On an ordinary spring afternoon in 1967, I was sitting on a curb on Telegraph Avenue in Berkeley, California, carefully peeling a pink grapefruit I had just purchased from the health-food store behind me. In about an hour, I would walk, with the help of a cane, down to Harmon Gymnasium to continue my strength-building and rehabilitation program. I was recovering from a badly broken leg, which I had injured in a motorcycle crash a few months before.

I was twenty-one years old, beginning my senior year of college. In that moment, though, I wasn't thinking of past or future—I was just peeling that grapefruit, sitting on that curb, in a kind of peaceful reverie, watching the wheels of various cars drive by, noticing pieces of litter blowing in the street, and life was okay.

In the next instant, something happened. No sounds, visions, or angelic choirs marked the occasion—yet in an instant, my life shifted as I looked up and noticed that *everything was perfect*. This "noticing" wasn't an insight or idea or thought or belief or experience but a radical shift in worldview, a perceptual break-through, unearned and unasked for. This moment of grace arrived in an unguarded moment, in the space of a single breath.

Prior to this rather odd and spontaneous awakening on Telegraph Avenue, if I had heard the phrase, "It's all perfect," I might have thought it a good bumper sticker, mantra, or affirmation. But in those moments of openness, that whispered revelation struck like silent thunder with the force of a tidal wave of transparent truth that turned my life around.

In the decades that would follow, I'd have various experiences generated by fasting, immersive spiritual practices, deep contemplation, and meditation—rising bliss, insights about the nature of mind and the universe, a sense of unity with all things. But none of those experiences came close to my awakening to the certainty that *everything was perfect exactly the way it was.*

The exhaust coming from the cars driving by—*perfect*; the litter blowing in the street—*perfect*; my broken leg now healing—*perfect*; the people walking by—*all perfect just the way they are.* I embraced the whole of creation the way a mother might embrace her child.

If a mugger had attacked me in that moment, it would have been absolutely perfect—and my response would have been too, whatever it might have been. Life no longer had any "wrong" choices—every single one would lead to evolution and wisdom.

I remained aware that, as I sat on the curb, a war was raging in Vietnam, and people everywhere were experiencing joy and despair, life and death, pleasure and pain. Yet I was *incapable* of seeing, thinking about, perceiving, or imagining anything in creation as less than *the perfect process of life unfolding.* I *knew* with a certainty beyond anything I had ever known that all was exactly as it should be and was happening for our highest good and ultimate well-being.

There's a story about Sir Laurence Olivier, who, after giving a mesmerizing, stunning performance on stage, stormed into his dressing room and slammed the door. A friend looked inside and said, "Larry, why are you so angry? What happened out there—what you did—was amazing!"

"Yes," Sir Laurence responded in frustration, "but I don't know what I did or how to repeat it!"

As time passed, the immediacy of my curbside realization faded. I forgot, then I remembered, then I forgot again, as we all do. There were times I yearned to recapture the clarity of that original revelation. But like Sir Laurence, I did not know what I had done or how to make it happen again. And I wasn't about to start a spiritual path founded on curb sitting or grapefruit peeling. Some moments of light simply come by grace to touch us, heal us, and change us.

Those moments of all-pervading perfection, however, continue to inform my awareness. I no longer take myself or the world quite as seriously, no matter what the circumstances may be. Even as the roller-coaster ride and drama continues, there remains an underlying sense of equanimity and perspective.

My words may offend those who say, "Easy for you to talk—you were a young athlete, a successful, relatively comfortable middle-class American. What about families living in war zones, what about people who are desperately ill, what about mothers holding starving infants while you share how it's all *perfect*?" And that is a fair and important question.

There are indeed many souls in need of help and nurturance—any one of us could recite an endless litany of injustice and human suffering. Consider the Serbian proverb, "Two men looked out of prison bars; one saw mud and the other saw stars." Both mud and stars, darkness and light, exist in this world.

Nonetheless, no matter what our immediate experience of life, the human psyche can move between two realities: the conventional and the transcendental. Conventional reality is comprised of the stuff of everyday consciousness and the dualities of daily life, where death is real, we are separate beings, and accidents happen. But when our awareness touches the transcendental, we *see*, as I saw on that curb years ago, our eternal life, essential unity, and innate perfection in a universe in which there are no accidents. As Einstein realized, "God does not play dice with the universe."

This state of awareness is not simply the domain of the comfortable or middle class—it also visits those souls who are dying, imprisoned, and in the direst of circumstances.

Perhaps it was in such a transcendent moment that Shakespeare wrote, "All the world's a stage, and all the men and women merely players ..." Each time this awareness comes to me, I smile with understanding and compassion for all of us. I remember once again that life is a game we play as if it matters and that each moment is sacred and unfolding perfectly as it is.

40

PARKER J. PALMER

Palmer is founder and senior partner of the Center for Courage and Renewal, which offers long-term retreat programs to help teachers, physicians, clergy, and others to "rejoin soul and role." His most recent books are A Hidden Wholeness: The Journey Toward an Undivided Life; The Courage to Teach: Exploring the Inner Landscape of a Teacher's Life; *and* Let Your Life Speak: Listening for the Voice of Vocation. *For more information, visit www.courage renewal.org.*

Fifteen years ago, I was hiking solo in the high desert at the foot of the Sangre de Cristo Mountains near Taos, New Mexico, when I was overwhelmed by a sudden realization that the universe is utterly indifferent to me and, at the same time, profoundly forgiving and compassionate toward me. I remember stopping and just standing in that knowledge for a long time. I had a simple and quiet sense of, *Oh, I get it. I see who I am, where I am, and how I fit into things.* I felt joy and lightness, as if my burdens had been taken from me. Talking about it almost distorts it. There are experiences that go far beyond words, and this was one of them.

I can't say that this experience changed my life, but it gave me an important lens through which I've looked at my journey ever since. A few years ago, I was reading a journal by Thomas Merton in which he reports his great revelation that "everything is emptiness and everything is compassion." And I thought, *That's it! That's the same experience I had!*

Of course, this experience is paradoxical—how can indifference and compassion coexist? I'm reminded of a Hasidic tale where the rabbi says to his disciple, "Everyone needs a coat with two pockets. In one pocket, carry dust to indicate that you are nothing. In the other pocket, carry gold to indicate that you are precious." We shrug off the burden of the self-obsessed ego by realizing that we are nothing, and we transcend self-denigration by realizing that there is something of ultimate value about each of us.

When I feel connected to spirit, there's a great sense of release and peace and yet also a great sense of aliveness and energy. Though it's peaceful, there's nothing passive about it—it's a call to deeper engagement with life. Genuine spiritual experience inevitably leads us back into the world, I think—back into works of love and mercy and justice—with new freedom, new clarity, and new power.

41

JIM PETERSEN

Petersen, a television analyst for the NBA's Minnesota Timber-
wolves, played eight seasons for the Houston Rockets, Sacramento
Kings, and Golden State Warriors. His best year as a professional
came during the 1986–87 NBA season as a member of the Rockets,
when he averaged 11.3 points per game. Jim can be reached at
jpetersen@timberwolves.com.

I read *Autobiography of a Yogi* by Paramahansa Yogananda when
I was with the Golden State Warriors, toward the end of my
basketball career. Yogananda had founded a religious organization
called Self-Realization Fellowship (SRF) in 1920, and his book
made such an impression on me that I decided to check out a
service at an SRF temple if I ever had the chance.

In 1993, the year after I retired, I moved to San Diego to complete my degree in sports psychology at San Diego University for
Integrative Studies. While I was looking for a place to live, I
stayed at the Doubletree Hotel in San Diego.

One Saturday, an ex–NBA teammate of mine named Alton
Lister came to town for a visit, and he and I went for a workout at
The Sporting Club at the Hyatt Regency in La Jolla. In the locker
room afterwards, Alton was bragging about how great his son and
daughter were. I wasn't married and had no prospects at the time,
but I said that if I ever had a daughter, I know that she would have
me wrapped around her finger. This guy next to me, a complete
stranger, said, "You don't know how right you are." Alton and I

were taken aback, but he looked like a friendly guy, so I chatted with him for a few minutes before I went back to the hotel.

The next morning, I was able to go to an SRF temple for the first time. I had asked the general manager of the Doubletree Hotel if she had ever heard of SRF, and she said, "Yes, there's a temple just north of us in Encinitas." She expressed a desire to go with me, so off we went. Brother Ramananda gave the service, and it was phenomenal. He really inspired me.

After the service, we decided to go to a restaurant called L'Auberge right down the coastline in Del Mar. We walked in, and lo and behold, the guy I had seen the day before, whose name was Paul Friedman, was sitting at a table with some other folks. He introduced me, among others, to a guy named Mike Flynn, the general counsel for SRF, and a woman named Ophelia, who was an assistant to Deepak Chopra.

It turned out that Paul knew all of the SRF monks and was very connected with Mother Center, the SRF headquarters located at Mount Washington in Los Angeles. After this second chance encounter, Paul and I decided we absolutely needed to be friends.

The next weekend was the final commemoration of Yogananda's hundredth birthday. There was a big celebration at Mother Center, so Paul took me up to Mount Washington with his whole family. I knew virtually nothing about SRF, so Paul tried to give me some perspective on who all these people were as we were driving up to L.A.

Paul told me about Brother Anandamoy, a native of Switzerland who was an architect with Frank Lloyd Wright before becoming a direct disciple of Yogananda, who the devotees called "Master." Paul said, "If you happen to have an audience with Brother Anandamoy, you have to realize it will be like meeting one of Jesus Christ's disciples. To meet him is like meeting Master in a sense because he was blessed by being in Master's presence."

At Mother Center, I joined the line to view Master's bedroom, which was cordoned off. You can go up to the door and look into the room but you can't go into the room. Many devotees kneel down in front of his photograph, which is sitting on an easel inside the room. Now remember, at this point, I'm only a week into my SRF experience. I considered myself a Jesus Christ disciple, so kneeling down in front of this Indian yogi didn't feel altogether right.

After viewing Master's bedroom, I went back downstairs and started chatting with Paul on the veranda, and he introduced me to Brother Anandamoy. This was all such a whirlwind for me. Here I am, going from having no real knowledge about SRF to visiting Mother Center, meeting all these blessed souls, and chatting with monks who were direct disciples of Yogananda. I was able to talk to Brother Anandamoy for four or five minutes.

That conversation with Brother Anandamoy was when my heart changed. Meeting him was truly an epiphany. Kneeling down in front of Master didn't make sense one second, and then the next second, it did. It wasn't even anything Brother Anandamoy said. It was just being in his presence; it was his energy, his peacefulness. He had that special something that those who have meditated and given their life to God in a very real way have, and I wanted it too.

Just shaking Brother Anandamoy's hand was transformative in and of itself. Whatever way he did it, he was able to transfer his peacefulness into me. And it changed my life forever.

42

BERNIE SIEGEL, M.D.

Dr. Siegel, a former surgeon whose book, Love, Medicine and Miracles, *catapulted him to the forefront of the mind-body-spirit revolution, founded the Exceptional Cancer Patients support group near his home in New Haven, Connecticut. His latest books are* Love, Magic, and Mudpies; 365 Prescriptions for the Soul; *and the children's book* Smudge Bunny. *For more information, visit www.berniesiegelmd.com and www.ecap-online.org.*

The biblical story of Abraham and Isaac has always been difficult for me to accept because the idea of sacrificing one of my children is so unthinkable. Well, ten years ago, I had some experiences that gave me a deep appreciation of that story. While talking to a friend on the phone about my travel schedule, she asked, "Why are you living such a busy life?" I suddenly and literally went into a trancelike state and saw myself with a sword in my hand, killing people. The same thing happened again a month or two later as I was sitting in an airplane looking out the window. It felt like I was watching a movie with me as the main character. I was a knight, and my lord told me that I was to kill the neighbor's daughter because the neighbor had been imposing on my lord's land. I agreed to do it out of fear that I would be punished if I refused. I learned where the daughter slept, but when I walked into her room with my sword drawn, she awakened and turned toward me. I saw my wife's face, yet I went ahead and killed her. I can't tell you how emotional that was for me. I brought her head back to my lord and said, "Are you happy now? Look what you've done!"

And he said, "I didn't do it; you did. If you had had faith in me, there would have been another result."

I was very concerned about these visions, so I sought the help of James Hillman, a Jungian therapist whose name kept popping up in articles I was reading. Since he lived in Connecticut, I drove up to see him. I started telling him what happened, and he said, "Wait a minute, are you listening to what you're saying? You keep talking about the lord."

I said, "Well, it's the lord of the castle."

"No, it's more than that," he said. "It's the Lord." We then discussed the story of Abraham, and when I re-read the Bible story after the session, I saw with great clarity that Abraham, who offered no resistance to God, and Isaac, who offered no resistance to his father, both had tremendous faith and knew that God would not allow Abraham to commit such a terrible act. The key question was this: Are you listening to and following the true Lord or an artificial one? I realized that when you truly follow the Lord, then everything you do will enhance your life, and just like Abraham, you'll feel an angel's hand on your shoulder to keep you from doing any harm. When you have faith in your Lord, you simply say, "Yes, I will go."

Soon after that, I had another episode where, again, my lord told me to kill the neighbor's daughter, and I said, "Fine, I'm going."

But this time I felt a hand on my shoulder, and my lord said, "Stop. Now that I know you have faith, bring them here so we can resolve this." Ultimately, my lord said that the way to resolve the dispute was to have his son (which he now called me because of my faith in him) marry the daughter because then we would be one family and there would be nothing to fight over. And that's what struck me, that the way to resolve the problem, and indeed any problem in the larger world, was to bring love to the situation and to become one family. And that's what I had to learn. I also intuitively knew that my career as a surgeon was in response to my need to heal with a sword rather than injure with one.

43

ESTHER M. STERNBERG, M.D.

Dr. Sternberg, the author of The Balance Within: The Science Connecting Health and Emotions, *is chief of the Section on Neuro-endocrine Immunology and Behavior at the National Institute of Mental Health. She is internationally recognized for her discoveries in brain-immune interactions and the effects of the brain's stress response on health—the science of the mind-body interaction. Recognized by her peers as a spokesperson for the field, she translates complex scientific subjects in a highly accessible manner, with a combination of academic credibility, passion for science, and compassion as a physician. For more information, visit www.esther sternberg.com.*

In the last months of my mother's struggle with breast cancer, I was writing an article for *Scientific American* magazine on the science of the mind-body connection. It focused on how the brain's stress response communicates with and changes the immune system and how those kinds of signals from the brain can contribute to illness by impairing the immune system's ability to fight disease. The article was very academic, very careful not to speculate and overstep any boundaries of what was actually proven with solid scientific studies.

I wrote and edited much of that article on a laptop by my mother's bedside in Montreal. I would frequently fly there from Washington to visit her. She would doze a lot, and when she would wake up, we would have discussions about what I was writing. She was very insistent that I not focus so much on how stress can make you sick. She said, "What about the belief part of it? You have to put something in there about how positive emotions can make you well."

I would argue with her that we didn't have enough proof—this was back in late 1996—that belief has any effect on health. She was a very feisty lady and maintained that I should include that piece in what I was writing. Well, of course I didn't, because that was not where the field was at the time or what my editor wanted.

It was during this period that I developed inflammatory arthritis. There's a long history of arthritis in my family, so it wasn't terribly surprising, but I believe it was not a coincidence that I developed this at a time when I was experiencing tremendous stress. Not only was my mother dying, but I had just moved to a new home and had just gone through some very difficult times.

I underwent some tests at the National Institute of Health— all kinds of space-age, sophisticated molecular biology and radiology studies to figure out what was causing this arthritis. I was supposed to go back into the hospital to try an experimental treatment, but my mother died so I put that off.

Soon after my article was published, I was asked to write a book on the science of the mind-body connection by the editor of the *Scientific American* book series. I had been researching the topic for many years, all the while attempting to stay on the academic high road. In the academic, scientific, and medical communities, the field carried a lot of baggage because it had been so enthusiastically embraced by popular culture for thousands of years, and there wasn't enough hard evidence to prove these connections.

It was ironic that the science of mind-body connection was not only ignored but actually rejected by the parent disciplines from which it sprang—immunology, endocrinology, and neuroscience.

We were skeptical, not so much about whether stress could make you sick, because there was a lot of research—including some key research that I had performed myself—that proved the connection between the brain's stress response and the immune response, but the other side of it—whether believing could make you well.

In the book proposal, my editor and I decided to include a chapter titled "Can Stress Make You Sick?" as well as a chapter called "Can Believing Make You Well?" The plan was to debunk the notion that believing could make you well, because there wasn't much solid research that proved that believing in anything in particular could help a person heal.

As I was writing the book proposal at my new house on a rainy March afternoon, my next-door neighbors, Tarja and Dean Pappavasiliou, rang the doorbell to introduce themselves, carrying moussaka and all kinds of delicious Greek food. When they asked me if I was a writer, I said, "I guess I am. I'm just starting to write a book proposal. Why do you ask?" They said they had always wanted a writer to stay at their cottage in Crete. I said, "Well then, yes, I guess you could call me a writer." And so I soon went with them to stay at their cottage, an experience that was life transforming.

The Pappavasilious' cottage was in a tiny, isolated village called Lentas on the south coast of Crete. It overlooks the Mediterranean and faces the border between Libya and Egypt. To reach it, you have to go over two chains of mountains and across the valley in the middle of Crete.

It was beautiful. I swam every day in the Mediterranean's wonderful, warm waters. Every day, even though I had difficulty walking when I first arrived there, I would climb to the top of a hill above the village, where there were the archaeological ruins of an ancient Aesklepion—a temple to Aesklepios, the Greek god of healing. The Greeks built many of these temples, always on the top of a hill overlooking the sea. People would come there to be healed with sleep, dreams, music, social support, lots of friends, a healthy diet, and exercise.

I would sit amidst the ruins and soak in the incredible view of the ocean, of the white stucco buildings with blue trim, and of the beautiful red and pink bougainvillea. It was the most soothing and relaxing time. I would sit there for hours, effectively meditating.

On top of the temple was a Byzantine church. And on top of that, there was a little Greek chapel, where the villagers came to place religious icons and candles. It was cool and dark and very soothing to sit there and look out at the ocean. I felt very peaceful. Another thing that was wonderful about that village was there were hundreds of grandmothers who all were happy to feed me with wonderful, healthy Greek food.

By the time I left Greece ten days later, I felt well again; I could climb up to the temple easily. When I returned home, I did not need to go back into the hospital or take any experimental treatments. At that point, I realized that there was a lot more to healing than simply medicine and space-age diagnostic tests. Those are extremely important, and of course I had been on medication to help my arthritis, but I had started that medication months before going to Greece and it hadn't been helping—until I went off and allowed my body to heal.

What I began to understand was that we've learned a great deal in medicine about ways to diagnose and heal disease. But it takes more than advances in medical disciplines to truly heal. You have to consider the whole body and the spirit. These space-age medicines will not do their job as well if you fight against them, if you continue to place yourself in stressful situations. You need to take yourself offline and combine those space-age treatments with the ancient knowledge that has been around for thousands and thousands of years—practices like meditation, prayer, exercise, and social support.

After my experience in Greece, the answer to that chapter on "Can Believing Make You Well?" became *yes*. Even if all the evidence wasn't in at that time, which was 1999, there was certainly enough there to begin to piece together the puzzle to say that yes, believing and participating in these salubrious activities can make you well, can help you heal. The turning point for me was when I began to merge the science I did with my own personal experience, my own personal and emotional life.

In writing the book, it was almost as if I was continuing that conversation with my mother at her bedside. And my answer to her with the book was, *Yes, you were right that believing can make you well*.

44

BARBARA J. WINTER

Winter, the author of Making a Living Without a Job *and Jump-start* Your Entrepreneurial Spirit, *is a self-employment advocate who travels the world encouraging and inspiring people through her writing and seminars to choose their right livelihood. Her newsletter,* Winning Ways, *which helps readers "turn passions into profits," is now in its twenty-first year. For more information, visit www.barbarawinter.com.*

One sunny afternoon twenty years ago, when my daughter Jennie was ten, we set out to visit my parents' house in Santa Barbara, California, for an informal family gathering. Jennie was riding her bike, and I was walking along behind her on a little bicycle path. Two blocks into our mile and a half walk, completely out of nowhere, an absolutely wonderful sensation just washed over me. It was an indescribable feeling of divine connection and an overwhelming sense of total peace. I can remember feeling filled with joy. It was like all my senses were heightened—the sunlight got even brighter, and I could smell the flowers more acutely than I ever had before.

And in that moment, I also had a deep sense of knowing that everything was, and always has been, unfolding perfectly. That knowing was so intense and so real that it was almost like I heard a voice saying, *All is well.* I was so taken aback by all this that I stopped dead in my tracks and just let it all flow through me. It was everything I had ever read about transcendental experiences, the kind that people worked their whole life toward achieving, but I had no understanding of why it was happening or what triggered it.

We often think that mystical experiences are triggered by an extraordinary event. And it ain't necessarily so. It can be in the midst of what seems very ordinary. I was just on this ugly little bike path. It was so not the place you would think you would go to find nirvana.

The experience only lasted a couple of minutes, but the residual effects lasted for hours. We got to my parents' house and it was like I was in a different state of consciousness—I was sensing everything differently. My sister Margaret and I were playing Scrabble, and at one point I looked at her and said, "Oh, I see how come you're such a good Scrabble player; you can look at your tiles and rearrange them in your mind." She just looked at me like that was the oddest thing. But all of a sudden I understood that she did this differently than I did. I was having all these insights into the people around me, people I had known all my life. And it was very noticeable.

I remember Margaret looking at me and saying, "I don't know what you have, but I want it." I was just so blissful and peaceful. It was a state of grace. It's hard to verbalize how intense and profound it was.

I've heard people who have had similar experiences say that for the rest of their lives they try to get back to it, which I have never been able to do, except that ever since, I have always been able to remember in times of crisis that I knew everything was happening exactly as it should. And there's a real calm spot inside of me that I can come from. So even though I've never been able to recapture that heightened state, I can always draw on it.

45

VICTOR LEMONTE WOOTEN

Regarded as the most influential bassist since Jaco Pastorius, Wooten is known for his solo recordings and tours and as a member of the Grammy-winning supergroup Béla Fleck and the Flecktones. He is an innovator on the bass guitar as well as a talented composer, arranger, producer, vocalist, and multi-instrumentalist. His first novel, The Music Lesson: A Spiritual Search for Growth through Music, *is available through his website, www.victorwooten.com.*

I'm lucky to have grown up with very spiritual parents, both of whom came from very spiritual families. When my mom was growing up, for instance, everything from finding the right land to farm on to what wood to build their house with to the spot to actually build the house was all governed by my grandmother's dreams and visions.

My mother had the same gifts. I remember driving with one of my four brothers and getting pulled over by the police because our car fit the description of someone they were looking for. When the policeman saw that we were dressed in suits, he let us go. But my mom, who was three hours away in another state, called us on the phone right away asking us what happened. We grew up with those types of stories, thinking it was normal.

That's why a dream I had in the mid-'80s made such an impression on me. I dreamt that I was flying over my grandmother's front yard with a bunch of bright blue birds. I looked down and saw my mom standing in the front door, telling me to get inside because a storm was coming. I remember being surrounded by these birds and knowing that I was okay, that I was protected. I tried to tell my mom that I was fine, but she was really worried and kept trying to get me to come down from the sky and come inside. I knew it was a special dream because I rarely dream in color. Still, I didn't really know at the time what the dream meant.

Later that year, I was patrolling with a crime-prevention group called the Guardian Angels in Virginia. We had stepped in and broken up a fight between two girls, but the crowd standing around watching did not want the fight broken up. So the crowd and the girls all turned on us. I was the patrol leader and there were only seven of us, three of whom were new recruits. I knew we had to retreat, but I didn't want to just take off running because that would excite the crowd and make them come after us even harder. So we just started walking away, but the crowd followed us, throwing rocks and getting more vocal and violent by the minute.

I had one of my team members, a woman named Cathy, in one hand and another member named Aaron in the other. Aaron was getting mad and wanted to retaliate, but I kept dragging them, saying, "We've gotta go, we've gotta go." After we finally reached safety in a nearby convenience store, I realized that one of our members was missing. I took off my red beret and my white Guardian Angels T-shirt so I wouldn't be easily identifiable and went back out through the crowd looking for him.

The thing that was really interesting about that night is that at no time was I concerned for my own safety. I just wanted to get my group out of there safely. Cathy, who I'm still good friends with today, later said that people were hitting me with sticks as I was dragging her and Aaron along, and I don't remember that at all. Not only that, but the member who had gotten separated from us ended up calling my house and asking my mom if she had heard from me, which was a huge mistake. That really freaked my mom out, thinking that something had happened to me. So she was calling me, and I'm telling her not to worry, that everything's fine.

And then I remembered my dream. Just like in that dream, my mom was worried and calling me, and I was telling her I was okay. I knew that I was safe, that I was totally surrounded by God—there's really no way not to be. That's why, even though the crowd had been threatening us, I was so not concerned with my own safety—it wasn't even a thought. I just knew I had to protect my group of people.

That incident led to a very powerful clarification dream. I was in Germany on a European tour in the mid-'90s. In my dream, I was at a party. It wasn't at my house, but I was in charge. My goal was to make sure that everyone at the party was taken care of and happy. There were only men at the party, and I was going around asking if everyone was okay, if anybody needed anything. People were making requests—I can remember certain people asking for women. I knew that whatever people asked for, I could get. But it was my responsibility to make sure that anything that was granted to them was used responsibly. If it was women, it was just for the female energy, the companionship, and not for sex.

In order for me to get something that was requested, I had to pick up a receiver, sort of like a telephone, that would make a direct connection to what I would call God, even though no terminology was used in this dream. I would have to pick up the receiver and whisper an oath that nobody else was allowed to hear. Basically, the oath was stating that I was going to be totally responsible for the request. At the end of the party, I was given a gift while a voice rang in my mind that said, *This one is for you.* It was the same voice that I had been speaking to on the receiver.

When I woke up, I called my mom and grandmother to tell them about the dream and ask for their interpretation. They were very happy about it and told me that the purpose of the dream was to help me see what my role in life is. And I do see now that the role I've taken on in life is to help take care of people and to help make good things happen for them. The dream also clarified for me that, in whatever I do for people, I have to be responsible for my actions, even to the point of taking on part of the responsibility for what *they* do with it.

Then, in 2000, I ran my first music camp for bass players. I call it a bass/nature camp because we teach nature awareness and how to use the outdoors and nature to enhance whatever it is we do in life. Since it was essentially a music camp, I wasn't sure how people were going to take to it because we do a lot of spiritual-type exercises, many of which are done blindfolded, like eating meals and walking in the woods. On the last day, we were walking around the camp as people were packing up to leave. A young teenager came over to me with tears in his eyes and said, "You know, Victor, when I first got here, I was looking around going, "Oh my God, there goes Victor Wooten! But now I see *everybody* that way."

It was at that point when I realized that we did it; this was exactly what we were after. To hear this young, macho teenage boy with tears in his eyes come to me and say that at a music camp—I thought, *Wow, we really pulled off something amazing.* He got a whole lot more out of camp than just how to play his instrument. I started crying and gave him a big hug. Then I got all the instructors together and told them what had just happened. I thanked all of them and hugged them too.

I use the oath from my dream to this day. And I've found that I've been able to, for lack of a better term, help people find themselves through the talent that I've been given, which is music. Especially through these camps, I've been able to use music to help people grow and find themselves. And I have grown so much from it too. I've been able to find my own self and answer questions about my own life through helping others.

Closing Thoughts

These stories have inspired me and become part of me. I hope they had the same effect on you. I often find myself thinking about them as I'm going through my day. Whether I'm faced with a particularly daunting challenge, meeting a friend for dinner, or simply counting my blessings, I imagine these storytellers cheering me on, encouraging me to seize the day, challenging me to reach out to others in friendship and love.

This book was a labor of love. Looking back, I marvel at how effortlessly all the many pieces of it fell into place. I'm glad I can share it with you. I only wish that I could share it with my dad. If that sounds like a lead-in to one more story, you're right.

Three years ago, my first book was published. It was a business book, and I brought it to St. Cloud, Minnesota, to give a copy to my mom. On my way back home to Minneapolis, I stopped at the nursing home to see my dad. He was sitting in the day room in the Alzheimer's ward, waiting for lunch. Well, that's not entirely true; he wasn't waiting for lunch, or waiting for anything for that matter. He was just sitting at a table, slumped in his chair, his mouth hanging open, a vacant look in his eyes.

As usual, he didn't react when I walked over to him. I sat down and said, "Dad, I wrote a book. See, my name's on the cover." He stared blankly ahead. I told him that, all my life, whenever I wrote something I was proud of, he was the first person I wanted to show it to. And then something amazing happened—he started to cry. Hugging him, I told him that I knew he understood what I was saying and that it meant the world to me. He cried twice more before I left. Here I thought he had left us long ago, but somehow, some way, he had broken through the barrier of his ravaged mind to let me know that he was still in there and still proud of me. Three months later, he was gone.

That story touched me deeply, and I suspect it also resonates with you. All of us have lost loved ones and have either gratefully experienced or regretfully wished for some form of closure or farewell at the eleventh hour. Stories like mine, while deeply personal, are also universal; they strike a chord and reverberate in the hearts and minds of countless others. The details of their stories may be different, but the feelings, the emotions are the same.

All of us have stories that deserve to be heard. Sharing a story with others forges deep and lasting bonds and creates a sense of community. We may never meet the storyteller, but after reading just a few paragraphs, we feel like we know that person, like there's one more human being on the planet whom we can trust, whom we can share our vulnerabilities with.

I'd like to hear your story. If you're willing to share it, please send it to me via my website, www.sixtysecondsbook.com. Don't forget to bookmark the website and visit it often to catch up on all the powerful and poignant stories I'll be posting.

I'd also like to hear your thoughts about this book. Which stories did you like the most and why? Which stories could you have done without? Would you like to see another collection of such stories? I value and look forward to your feedback. Don't hesitate to fire off an e-mail to me at sixtyseconds@mac.com.

Thank you for your support and friendship—and for being a part of my story.